To Tina
with love a
Roy x

There's Nowt Like Wanting

An Unusual Education Autobiography

Roy Norcliffe

Bloomington, IN Milton Keynes, UK
authorHOUSE®

AuthorHouse™
1663 Liberty Drive, Suite 200
Bloomington, IN 47403
www.authorhouse.com
Phone: 1-800-839-8640

AuthorHouse™ UK Ltd.
500 Avebury Boulevard
Central Milton Keynes, MK9 2BE
www.authorhouse.co.uk
Phone: 08001974150

© 2006 Roy Norcliffe. All rights reserved.

No part of this book may be reproduced, stored in a retrieval system, or transmitted by any means without the written permission of the author.

First published by AuthorHouse 8/31/2006

ISBN: 1-4259-4684-4 (sc)

Printed in the United States of America
Bloomington, Indiana

This book is printed on acid-free paper.

Also by the same author: There and Back Again
First published 2000

Foreword

"Ambition, if it is to be savoured, let alone achieved, has to be rooted in possibility".

(P.D.James)

A wise old man I came across in the steel industry frequently said to me 'There's now't like wanting, you know'. He was referring to people he had come across in his life who simply didn't want to do something, or indeed oft times anything!.

I believe Bill had a point, and that it is remarkable what might be achieved if you do reach out for it. I trust this book reflects some example of Bill's simple philosophy.

The 11+ examination determined a childs' immediate educational future, either at Grammar School or the largely derided Secondary Schools. Unfortunately, we 11+ failures somehow felt inferior – social misfits – even though we outnumbered the top guns.

There is no doubt, however, that so many of us, by wanting it enough, didn't do too badly did we?

Dedicated

To all the pupils and students who enriched my life for over thirty years

Acknowledgements

I would like to thank all those people who crossed my path, and were an important part of my life in education. Without your contribution, little would have been achieved.

I also thank my sister, Jillian Moore, for her time and patience in helping me to unravel and clarify my writing. Thank you to my true and trusted friend, Roy Ashby, for his considerable patience, interest and excellent skills in the final tidying up of the manuscript, all done with great good humour.

Contents

Foreword — v
Dedicated — vi
Acknowledgements — vii

Chapter 1
An Educational Tale To Be Told — 1

Chapter 2
Infancy and Junior Memories — 7

Chapter 3
A Secondary Technical Affair — 13

Chapter 4
The Agony and the Ecstasy — 23

Chapter 5
College Days — 29

Chapter 6
"If a Man Means Well" — 35

Chapter 7
Comprehensively Enjoyed — 41

Chapter 8
A Change Is Not As Good As A Rest — 59

Chapter 9
Deighton Incorporated — 71

Chapter 10
An Indian Summer in Park Lane — 81

Chapter 11
'Bits and Bobs' — 91

CHAPTER I

An Educational Tale To Be Told

I begin this autobiography, not in the sense of achieving fame and fortune, but in the simplistic belief that there is here, an education tale to be told, and that in telling the story of my career, readers might discover that it is somewhat different. A variety of people have suggested that the story be told, believing that, not only does it bear telling, but it might also serve as some sort of inspiration to others and help in their realisation that you can often get what you want – if you want it badly enough!

I have already written one short book and this one is likely to be my last - I don't feel that I am an author in the real sense of the word, but I can recognise when there might be a tale or two on which to dwell. My theme is about "education'" – not simply the formal process, but all the bits in between which one either learns from life and from people, or simply doesn't.

I have often been labelled a "people person" - I'm not entirely sure what it really means, but it is a sort of comforting term. However, I do know that I am mainly at ease with the majority, seem to have time and patience with those less fortunate in life, and have the passionate dislike of, or even aggression, towards anyone who chooses to hurt, either mentally or physically, their fellow man.

I arrived on the scene in June 1936 amid the furore of Edward VIII's abdication, but to a warm and pleasant summer's day. I was born in a small gardener's cottage where Grandad was the gardener to a rich industrialist of the 1930s, and where Grandma was superbly managing a smallholding, mainly of pigs and around 1,000 head of poultry. Bennett Grange Cottage is today Bennett Cottage and the years have produced many changes but nothing can detract from the majestic panoramic views seen from that cottage; the first peaks of the Derbyshire hills being in sight and Sheffield's Mayfield valley below with its woods, farmland and chequered patchwork of fields. Thankfully this has scarcely changed, even to this day. Thank heavens for being born the Yorkshire side of the border. Much as I loved our easy access to beautiful Derbyshire, the prospect of being anything other than a 'Tyke' fills me with dismay.

Perhaps it was here that the beginnings of calm, the influences of simplistic country values and customs took a grip. Sadly I can't remember Grandad but I remain convinced that much of his soul is within me. Whilst he died within three years of my birth, the photographs taken at the time easily show the depth of love and pride I engendered in him.

Grandmother was magnificent in every sense of the word, and to this day I could not find a blemish in her character. She possessed, above all else, gentleness and wisdom, was unstinting in her care of others, hardworking beyond belief, certain of her husband's place in heaven, and of her joining him there in the course of time.

She it was who told me that swallows gather on the roof of the barn in late September to travel thousands of miles south, then return, ducking and diving, the following spring time. Only when I travelled to North Africa and Southern Spain did I realise the magnitude of the achievements of my favourite winged creature.

On the other hand she taught me to hate and despise magpies because of their predatory instincts, and their constant desire to kill and not necessarily to feed – especially when Grandma's chicks were the hapless victims. Quite regularly farmers would hang out dead magpies as a warning to 'keep away'.

I stayed many times at Bennett Grange Cottage as a child, loving being in contact with the numerous animals there, and dealing with the primitive facts of life faced almost daily. The primitiveness, which I now find quite horrendous, was at the time acceptable and a realistic part of the daily social life and country culture.

Chickens and rabbits were perpetually cut of throat, and chopped behind their neck respectively, to provide food for family and for local buyers. I watched fascinated the plucking and dressing of these prospective tasty table dishes, Grandma wearing her plucking apron, completely covered in feathers and down – the cats waiting for any droppings or morsels that were of eatable quality, me quite open mouthed at the frenzy and speed of it all. Neutering of cats was unheard of seventy years ago hence any new arrivals found at birth were dispatched by drowning and then deposited on the muck heap where all the muck went – pig, poultry and human. Yes, we had an earth toilet, which no environmental or council employees emptied in those days – it was all DIY. Exactly where tin cans and household items went, I cannot recall - the newspapers were cut into quarters and hung in the toilet for unsophisticated bum usage.

The rate of decomposition of this heap was stupendously fast. Each year the whole ungodly muck and mess was spread back onto our smallholding land to promote potatoes, cabbage, carrots, turnips etc. These eventually grew into huge sizes and were of a rich quality. Certainly today they would win their respective sections in any village show or even the Yorkshire show. There were no signs of any dead kittens, the Sheffield Star remnants, or other unmentionables – it had all truly disappeared. Composting at its very best!

All this of course taught me an enormous amount, mainly that my rural experiences were vastly different from that of my contemporaries in the village where I lived – Ecclesfield. Maybe this wasn't entirely modernised, but my home and situation certainly were. I loved to adjust from running water and sanitation to a beloved alternative where water was drawn daily from a well about fifty yards away, and this is a sobering food for thought.

Once and once only did I feel my Grandmother's wrath. I had been playing in the yard, fallen and damaged a leg. I must have muttered some City oaths and foul language because she said reprovingly "God wouldn't like that".

"Then bugger God" – I rapidly responded, whereupon she cracked me so hard she literally knocked me to the ground. I was absolutely mortified. Firstly that she had actually, for the first and only time, raised her hand to me and that secondly, she had shown me that she could be hurt and offended like anyone else.

She was so religious that she never played cards, dominoes, or knit on a Sunday. Neither could we children. She allowed the adults to play but would only watch, and never play herself.

Mum used to have a regular New Year's Eve party, mainly involving games of Whist and other card games. She would patiently sit until the New Year dawned – with it a Monday – and then play until 3am in the morning. Conversely she would cease playing immediately before midnight and then just as patiently watch the participants when New Year's Day fell on a Sunday.

Her worship took her to a mission hut each Sunday - some three miles round trip. Her nearest Anglican church was a four miles round trip, and her trek to whist drives would often involve walks of even greater distances. Her strength right to the end was incredible, and I've seen her carry two full buckets of coal two or three times a day in her eighties – from coal house to fireside.

I was constantly learning from all these rich experiences and often joined her on what I affectionately termed her "scraps" round. This was usually once a week, winter and summer, where we pushed a large, if battered, baby pram around the houses of the gentry and middle-classes situated about a mile away. We collected anything in the way of food discards which could, in turn, be boiled, then mixed with meal and fed to her poultry, the few pigs by this time having been permanently disposed of. We began this trek around 5 am in the morning and it also involved some social chat and plenty of tea drinking. This was a steep learning curve for me in terms of class distinction – although Gran. had so much class herself.

Gran's background is still a mystery to me. I know she worked in service in Lincolnshire, overcame the stigma of having an illegitimate child, left school at 11 years of age, became a mid-wife and someone who, at the other end of life, could lay-out the dead – all self-taught! She was multi-skilled and in today's educational climate would surely have been most successful. She was, however, extremely competent at virtually anything she turned her hand to.

She was also extraordinarily beautiful as a young and middle-aged woman, the numerous family photographs proving this. I suppose many of us live with the regret of not being more inquisitive about our Grandparent's lives, their mistakes and the stories they could tell, until – regrettably – it's all too late.

Gran. eventually left Bennett Grange in 1948 – I got a day off school to help her move into an old people's complex on the edge of the city. I stood holding her hand as we stood at the top of the path.

"Goodbye old house" she breathed. At Bennett Grange, there had been so much happiness and many memories of the best sort.

Eventually Grandma passed away in my parents' home aged 84 and the last time I saw her was New Year's Eve 1962. Senility had set in and she was busy "baking mince pies" sat up in bed, her nightie in disarray.

"Oh it's you, hello" she said as I settled her back down. I was totally distraught and she died a few days later. Distraught because I loved her strength, her mind sets, her ability to face life full in the face and to take it on. What a wonderful example she set for someone to carry forward into life.

Chapter 2

Infancy and Junior Memories

I recall that my infant school education was dominated by the war years and the impact that these self-same years had upon the schools, their learners and instructors; 'monsters' as some of these latter were subsequently remembered as my educational path, evolved. Not at that time, certainly, because their teacher behavioural patterns were considered the norm at that time, although their actions would be considered largely inviolate nowadays. The memory of those 'Micky Mouse' gas masks and the air raid shelters will stay forever in my mind.

Take Mr Mackay, a large fearsome Scot who I understand retired to the Highlands and lived to almost 100 years of age. He taught most subjects but was particularly famous as he stalked between desks, rapping any knuckles without due warning or real reason, indeed at his slightest whim. He read two books to us, "Treasure Island" and "Black Beauty, but never completed either. Why? He invariably fell asleep during his readings. We, his class, would look at each other in wide eyed wonderment and even as 9 year olds, would have the good sense to remain completely silent and be content to make rude gestures and signs to each other, throw paper balls etc. etc. thus allowing Mac. his indeterminate slumber.

It was quite regrettable really because he was an excellent reader but we never realised Jim Hawkins sailing out on his adventures, or Black Beauty threatened by fire. All this however for me was the paradox of the first insights into the world of literature, and a burning desire to read for myself the development and conclusion of these two wonderful books.

Another torment initiated by Mr Mackay happened on our football day. Two sets of shirts, red and white stripes depicting Sheffield United, and the blue and white of Wednesday would be placed on the great fireguard to air and warm for our match. For some reason however this didn't always proceed in the manner desired or, and often we wouldn't get out onto the playing field. Maybe it was too cold or wet for Mac. or maybe he'd fallen asleep again; however the inconsistencies and his ad-hoc diagnostic teaching skills were perhaps unique. If he was a kindly or humane man then it was never disclosed, maybe he was, maybe he wasn't, we never knew. I like to think that as a teacher, young people got the same "me" whether inside the classroom or out of it. I could never understand why so many teachers need to develop two utterly contradicting personalities. I've known staff in the classroom be feeble, disorganised and without kudos, yet these self-same people were organised, human dynamos when away from school. Conversely total fascists in the teaching environment, they were warm, generous, gifted human beings when out of it.

I remember Mrs Crossland, an admirable teacher, and a member of our village who I met only a year or so ago, now aged about 90. I was honestly able to say that whilst an infant scholar, I found her skills both inside and outside the classrooms were skills that I wanted to fully embrace when I formally took up teaching as a career – even though it was some thirty odd years later. Not surprisingly, Mrs Crossland went on to become a totally respected Headteacher in a nearby village school. Her unfailing encouragement, calmness, and ability to convince you that she really cared – and she did – were the essential ingredients of her teaching pie.

Of course there were others in both Junior and Infant school circles who possessed that touch of inspiration and magic. Those like our Infant School's Head whose hardness hid a heart as big as a bucket, and whose red hair tantrums with her charges didn't hide her concerns for our war-time threatened education. We went to school, perhaps a walk of about one and a half miles complete with regulation gas-masks and identity bracelets – forget these at your peril!

Every so often we would be escorted through what could be termed a large empty furniture van, the difference being that somehow mild toxic gas was the cargo, and the authorities needed to ensure that our gas masks met regulation requirements. What happened to the poor unfortunates if it didn't, I never actually discovered.

Cod liver oil, malted milk and other such delights were fed to us daily as we waited, mouths agape in a row, for the spoon to be inserted. I'm not entirely sure that it wasn't the same spoon for us all, which would explain the eagerness to be first in the queue. However I don't recall any of us suffering as a result of this apparent lack of hygiene. Lessons were interrupted too by regular air raid shelter drills. These shelters were huge contraptions that housed the whole of the school, and yes we did go there for real on many an occasion, although the Sheffield blitz was largely a night-time affair. After the war, the shelters became, if not exactly a breeding ground, certainly a venue for late Junior School sexual fumblings and snoggings before meeting their demise.

Being left by my mother at the age of five in the care of a girl called Margaret, from up the road, was another traumatic experience in the early 1940s. No nursery reception and an easing into school at this time. One minute you were at home, the next, for six hours or more, entirely in a foreign and frightening learning experience. I feel to this day for the mums who suffer such anguish when this happens even in these different times and despite the more sophisticated and sensitive approaches to school entry, which we are to be congratulated upon today. My Infant and Junior education was certainly not privileged. Old buildings, dilapidated toilets without proper plumbing, or doors (never mind locked ones), and an absence of toilet paper was the norm. Usually I just hung on until I got home, but I have been known to make do with a bit of fallen toilet roof slate. Our Junior School teacher for the final year lived in a salubrious part of town, and if she thought on, she would bring newspaper cut into squares to help out our vulnerable bottoms. Here was another stern, physical punisher who failed to either recognise or encourage my burgeoning writing and reading skills. I could do little else, hence the undignified embarrassment of being an 11+ failure – something I'll come to later in this book.

Memories will abide with me forever from these my days at Junior School, the first being the death of my paternal Grandmother. I didn't see quite so much of her, as she had umpteen Grandsons and several Granddaughters – unlike my uniqueness on the maternal side – thus I felt then that maybe I was not particularly special. One day as I left school a lad called Major Higgins said:

"Aye, thi Grandmother's deed today!".

"What?" I asked, nonplussed.

"Aye she deed reet theer" pointing to the bus stop directly adjacent to the playground.

This direct statement lacking both sympathy and sincerity but delivered almost as a proclamation is something I can never forget – from the mouths of babes - and why didn't my teachers know?

I "galloped" home smacking my bum as either Roy Rogers on "Trigger", or Gene Autry on "Champion" to find Mum washing the windows with a tear-stained face. I knew it was indeed true. Grandmother Norcliffe, on the way to see her newly born Granddaughter had walked up the very steep hill from the bungalow in which she lived, and collapsed and died from a heart attack at the bus stop. Whilst I didn't spend much time with this Grandma she did on occasions feed me when Mum, now a heavy diabetic, needed hospital treatment on certain days.

Another 'gallop' home shortly afterwards saw me greeted by Grandma Richards with the words - "I think your Mum is going to go to Jesus".

I went to Mum's bedside where various relatives had gathered, all waiting for the ambulance, which hadn't come, or for her to die. Then I soberly returned to school. Call it what you will, and explain it how you might, but during the afternoon I had the enormous knowledge that she would be fine. She was, and came home some days later after suffering a deep diabetic coma. The third time I really galloped home was when I desperately, desperately, wanted the toilet and had refused the delights of the school ones. As I jumped the small stream however still half a mile from home – it happened. The extreme movement only succeeded in making my bowels move further. I had messed my pants, short trousers, socks and shoes too, actually. My galloping horse became a wide legged, limping, messy donkey of sorts.

I arrived home to Mum to be roundly, berated, cuffed around the ear and shamed. At the ensuing din, all three neighbours popped their heads out of their doors.

"What on earth's up, Elsie?" asked Mrs Stennett.

In a voice like thunder, and heard, I was sure, all the way to Barnsley. Mum exclaimed "Aye, it's our Roy – he's shit hisself"

CHAPTER 3

A Secondary Technical Affair

Secondary modern in the 1940s was universally disparaged and compared most unfavourably to its academic contemporary the Grammar School. Maybe the differences were over exaggerated; certainly many Secondary Schools were models of care, enthusiasm and teacher commitment. Secondary Schools were full of boys and girls who had not reached some arbitrary ability level at the age of 11 – that's all! That they might have reached this level weeks, months or years afterwards seemed never to be a consideration. Yet ultimately, as a teacher, I saw so many young people – as classic late developers – achieve standards at least equal, if not often superior, to their Grammar School counterparts. I was just such an example so I think I know what I'm expounding.

'Failure' at 11+ was a stigma, which affected many children before its eventual and proper abolishment, and that same sense of failure took some shaking off within oneself, before confidence was restored and hope returned. Inevitably, young people had particularly precious gifts and skills, which could be nurtured and developed as time went by.

There was some savagery however and I quote two examples whilst I was at Secondary School. The first details an English teacher (who was fearsome, and certainly not a pretty face) the second the Headmaster at the time. I could, but won't put real names to these people in case their relatives should read this book.

Mrs Stenson was in the habit of calling you to her desk where you had to present your work for inspection. By this time (2nd Year) I really knew that my writing skills were seriously developing but my presentation – alas as now – was less good. My presented English work to this teacher had the shame of a blot – remember no biros in 1948, but ink and pen; therefore it was very easy to mar the work's content.

"What a mess, Norcliffe" she shrieked, hushing the class instantaneously, "Why don't you wipe your shoes on it lad?"

Now I didn't give this a second thought because she had actually thrown the exercise book at my feet, and without ado, did as she had suggested. The outraged woman, now in danger of suffering an apoplectic fit, or worse, then proceeded to throw the whole caboodle through a partly opened window – her aim was masterly – and in its descent of ten or twelve feet it totally disintegrated. To make matters worse the playground below was wet, and the book, almost full of writing, which I had proudly collated, was a wreck. My pride and joy virtually destroyed! I was mortified and heartbroken, believing still that this was to be the most significant piece of humiliation I ever suffered at school. I could never forget or forgive my humiliation. Perhaps I was fortunate that nothing worse happened even though I did receive the cane at this establishment. The same dragon later accused me of copying when in fact my "friend" sitting next to me had copied my work. Perhaps the fact that his Dad was an M.D., and mine was a miner influenced her opinion.

I will briefly mention the corporal punishment because this was inflicted by a run-of-the-mill music teacher, not a Head or Deputy, simply because I couldn't (still can't) read the notes to music. Thus both these punishments were not for misdeeds but certain inabilities, however, the fact that senior staff were able to cane young people, without being truly aware of the facts, was another issue I found hard to come to terms with.

One day, a warm summer's one, the whole school were summoned in haste to assemble in the large playground. We curiously lined up to see two scruffy looking lads, recent arrivals from the City who had been bombed out of their homes and moved into the new sprawling adjacent council estate, being literally pulled across the yard, then hauled onto a raised concrete dais. The Headteacher, Mr Armitage, was blood red with rage and to our horror began beating the two boys about the body. No, it wasn't just a beating, it was a merciless thrashing in front of several hundred onlookers. The whole school was stunned, and frightened - it was like something from another age, another culture certainly, and not in keeping with the image of a Rural Secondary modern. That day something was instilled in me for ever, i.e. the evils of punishment being metered out by someone totally out of control and getting undoubted stimulus from their power, and the access this power gave them to behave in such a way. The boys' crime by the way? They had been caught stealing two carrots from the canteen's sacks of carrots placed outside. Their reason was that they were simply hungry. I have no doubt that such a cruel action today would lead to criminal proceedings and imprisonment, but hitting kids seemed to be merely a way of life in schools. Regularly the ruler over the knuckles was the only visible form of encouragement.

There were good teachers though. Mr Senior the Science teacher recognising some ability in my make-up with respect to plants and gardening was full of quiet and positive encouragement. The P.E. teacher too, a beautiful woman of real shape, would be most supportive in an area that wasn't my best by any means. Imagine what transports of delight, when she made us all lie on the floor and then walked slowly over us with very wide legged shorts. The view was enchanting and I don't think we'd been instructed to close our eyes! These were the routine sexual awakenings at this time, somewhat later in life than nowadays, but still real enough. I had begun to keep rabbits and decided to mate them to create babies, but Dad insisted that we boys – my best mate Adrian and I – leave the shed while he did the business.

There was such a commotion and we listened at the door as one hell of a fight broke out between the two creatures. Dad managed to pull them apart utterly perplexed – after all didn't rabbits have the best sexual connotation of all God's creatures? Ah, but you see, they were both females! The new addition, we had been informed, was a buck rabbit. How wrong can you be! Two doe rabbits don't make babies. Dad later left it to us to do the mating and another pal, later to reach a very powerful Director's post, was always insistent on being told when the Sunday morning matings were on the agenda.

Ronnie Hearne, sadly an early aged victim of the then unknown motor neurone disease, was the first to teach us about sex.

"Do you know that men insert their thingies between a woman's legs to make babies?" Ronnie duly informed us one day as we played by the stream.

"What, don't be daft - that's stupid" we told him. Still laughing we rode home on our bikes and I told my Mum. She didn't say a word, just looked at me in a very strange way; therefore I had to conclude that there must be something in it. My Dad on the other hand was so puritanical it was untrue. One day I heard the rhyme:

Thee, me and us two we met a lass.

Thee, me and us two we laid her in the grass.

Thee, me and us two we lifted up her clothes.

Thee, me and us two (two noises here) tha noas.

(Has to be said in Sheffield dialect).

I delighted in repeating this ditty to my Aunty Frances who lived next door. She was in stitches as I related this to her; and she was so broad-minded compared to my Dad, her younger brother. However my Dad happened to walk into the room just as I was finishing my party piece.

"Hey Jim, just listen to our Roy's poem" encouraged Aunty Frances.

I delightedly, and gleefully, wallowing in the attention I was getting, repeated.... "Thee, me" etc. The next thing I knew was being knocked for six straight over Aunty's settee and onto the hearth-rug. I knew then that all the sex stories, all the nudge nudges, and winks were indeed true. I'd arrived!

Whilst my 11+ examination was initially cancelled because of the massive 1947 snowfalls in the North, my 13+ scholarship exam day duly arrived and I had to travel to Barnsley for this. It was a total bolt from the blue when I learned that I had actually passed this, entirely I'm certain, because of my burgeoning writing skills. Plans had already been made to apply to an agricultural college, and these plans hastily scrapped. Wait for it, I was going on an engineering course – me, full of books, plays, plants and a love of the land, was going to be an engineer! What a laugh, what a joke!

Before I left this school I was asked to play David Copperfield in selected excerpts from Dicken's book. I only did this because the first choice, a local farmer's lad was indisposed. He wasn't best pleased when he returned to find I had stolen his role.

Whilst I had appeared on several Wesley Chapel May Queens from being an infant through to 1949, this was my first taste of "theatre" – little did I realise the significance of these first tentative attempts at acting. It was therefore with very mixed feelings that I began my Technical education in the faraway land of Barnsley with its mining heritage. Danny Blanchflower, and Tommy Taylor perhaps, at that time its major claim to fame. Michael Parkinson emerged a little later.

My school reports throughout had mainly, read 'Roy always tries his best' or 'Roy works really hard in school'. What they didn't say, and I bet they really wanted to, was 'but he's not that bright, a bit dim really, but always with the exception of English!' I perpetually believe that it was this single skill which, against all the odds, got me that Technical School scholarship.

However, the nightmare began again, and I was, as always, in the bottom three or four of the class, with the exception of English of course. Then something happened which I honestly believed changed my whole opinion of myself and proved an important educational point. Without anyone being really aware of what they'd done – I was moved to the next class down. Suddenly and totally unexpectedly, I was becoming top or next to the top in all subjects; at last I was in the right division for me and what an impact this had on my confidence and self belief. Alright, maybe I wasn't among the cream, but I was a darned sight better than a large number of people. I have hung on to this premise throughout my life – it's often been key to career survival.

Whilst I had always been a strong ball player ultimately reaching good standards in football, cricket, tennis, squash and now crown green bowling I could never ever handle Physical Education. Handstands, somersaults and vaults were anathemas to me, and to be avoided at all costs.

One year the then Headmaster at Barnsley Technical School had the bright idea of reading out the results of the third year internal examinations. What followed was a list of subjects and successful names. Failure wasn't mentioned so it didn't matter much in the boring long list of names being announced. Except when it came to P.E.! For some dark and mysterious reason, the clown had to say "Coldwell and Norcliffe – failed!"

Coldwell was so fat he could scarcely walk and to be coupled with him was total ignomy. Schools were not famed for their psychological approaches and child-centred thinking in those days. What did some teachers learn at college? I also remember being taught the rudiments of ballroom dancing at this school in preparation for a Christmas party. Imagine a whole line of 15 year-old boys stretched across the main hall 'forward one, side two, together three,' as we desperately tried to negotiate the Waltz. I didn't do too badly, and was in fairly confident mood to tackle the job when the school's Christmas dance night duly arrived.

The music began for the opening Waltz and the second and third years sat around desperately wondering what would happen, when a Snowball Waltz was announced by our teacher/compere (for those of you ignorant of such matters, this is where a couple begin the dance proceedings. When the music stops, they split up and choose fresh partners, and thus the floor is quickly filled). Well it transpired that the Head Girl, a year or so older than me, had been instructed to find a partner to open the proceedings. This totally devine creature from my side of Barnsley wearing a white tight Angola sweater made a beeline – surely not for me – but horror of horrors, yes indeed, for me. So my first ever public dance began before a crowded audience, and I was totally bewitched by both her glamour and beauty, and stupefied by my feet getting it right, 'one forward, two side, together three'. In later years I wondered if it was my obvious good looks and charm which made her choose me or had some teacher prompted her: - "Get Roy Norcliffe, he can dance a bit".

Other teachers were stunning in their teaching approaches; Gus Bailiff, an ex tank sergeant took us for P.E.

"Don't trap your balls lads when you vault the box"

"Serves you right Chambers, you shouldn't let 'em grow so big!"

Gus was an inspirational teacher, who nearly, but not quite, coached me to GCE level in Chemistry and Physics.

Don Hepworth, a quiet effective inspirational English teacher brought out my English gifts in superb style. I was only good enough to take two GCEs, Lang. and Lit. and that in the first year of Technical Schools being allowed to take GCE exams, I was the first and only - therefore unique scholar - to pass both Language and Literature in 1952.

Don it was who wanted me to consider journalism or teaching as a career. Teaching me, what a joke?! However Barnsley Chronicle did want a Junior at the time of my leaving school, but if I had accepted the post, I would have travelled to Barnsley and back for six days a week, and been paying out more than I was bringing in! So the financial implications were not at all realistic. Michael Parkinson did take an identical Barnsley Chronicle Junior newspaper route at virtually the same time – say no more.

My emerging skills as an actor were allowed to flourish whilst at Barnsley, and the honour of reading the school's tribute in remembrance of the death of George VI, which followed a major reading at the previous Christmas service in a crowded church, were other memories of an increasing self-awareness and confidence.

In the third year of technical education, I was awarded my first ever academic prize, a Physics book for the most improved pupil in Year 3. I was so proud when collecting this at speech day, particularly so because Mum had travelled ten miles on the bus to be an equally proud member of the audience.

Leaving school decisions and choices now had to be considered. Mum and Dad, aware of the post war-time political situation, recommended a job in the steelworks where exemption often applied, and Dad didn't want me to follow his footsteps into the mines. I owe my parents a great, great deal for all the love, care and concern they spread around our family – constantly. However, whilst I accepted their choice, I should have followed my heart into the arts field. As a consequence a career in the steel industry began in July 1952.

CHAPTER 4

The Agony and the Ecstasy

My time in the steel industry was not a period with which I particularly want to dwell in this book, even if it took up some nineteen years of my life. A succession of ill paid jobs with actually only minimal progression as a reward, and some insight into management techniques, which were both dubious and often blatantly unfair, just propelled me rapidly towards an alternative – teaching – but this was a long time ahead.

My part-time jobs were numerous. A Drama Youth Tutor, a Theatre Critic for Sheffield Newspapers, a Community Drama Tutor for Sheffield Education Authority, were all posts which paid quite well, and mentally my day job became very much secondary to all else. I still did it as best I could, but with decreasing enthusiasm. As I say, it took nineteen years to get the 'day job' out of my system – as things turned out a great deal too long.

As soon as I began work in 1952 I played qualification catch-up by taking an ONC course in metallurgy which meant studying Physics, Chemistry and Mathematics. Mathematics was always tremendously difficult, but I encountered an enlightened mathematician who suddenly made Geometry, Algebra, Calculus and the rest blindingly obvious. He was a superb part-time teacher, but I question whether it was just his skills or the fact that at the same time my brain was developing sufficiently to now absorb mathematical concepts previously denied me. Perhaps it was a bit of both.

This educational period covered three nights a week for two years, after finishing work at 6.00pm. It was the norm in the 1950s to go to night school and this preceded day release, sandwich courses and F.E. College. Significantly these qualifications were enormously important twenty-one years later, and were my passport to an Honours degree course after a teacher-training course.

I briefly flirted with fame when I applied, and came within a whisker of landing a plum job with Radio Sheffield – local radio being in its infancy in the late 1960s. I successfully negotiated two interviews and a dummy run reading various news bulletins, and then handling record requests, only to finish second out of initially two hundred or so applicants. The job involved research, preparation, and airtime on a rotating three week shift system. Shifts were not a problem to me because I'd done all that for three years or so at a small special steel making company. By the way, the successful Radio Sheffield applicant lasted barely six months in the job – and it transpired that he was a teacher!

I have mentioned the nineteenth century management skills of some directors. Can I recall one specific incident? In 1960 with a sick wife and equally sick baby I rang work to say I couldn't come in that day because of my predicament. Fortunately, Father-in-Law came early the next morning to alleviate my situation, and matters medically did take a turn for the better.

Imagine my dismay when my pay being docked for this day off, denuded my paltry enough wage further. Needless to say I challenged this with the wages department, who in turn referred me to my Director – Mr Wolman.

Mr Wolman called me into his knee-deep carpeted office and told me that, because I'd been absent on 'somebody else's behalf,' I was not entitled to be paid.

I pointed out to him that I'd had about ten days illness in the previous eight years and that this was a good track record. I said I wanted my money and in fact I needed my money. He reluctantly agreed to pay me.

"Do you know Mr Wolman" I said as I turned in the doorway, "Anytime I need some compassionate time off, or indeed any time for someone else's needs, then it will always be me who has the illness. You've taught me a life-long lesson that, in this case, honesty and the truth doesn't pay".

In later years as a manager, I always preferred my staff to tell me the truth about any days off which could be questionable. I'm not sure that they always did, but I hope that I had sufficient sympathy when the need arose.

However something was stirring inside me and fate stepped in to hasten my massive career change. One evening, instead of allowing me to take the usual mid-week evening Drama class (which I shared jointly with another teacher called Sonia), the Head of Centre asked me to join him for coffee. Unbeknown to me he'd apparently already squared this with Sonia. He said he wanted to talk and when we were settled he came straight to the point.

"Roy, have you ever considered becoming a full time teacher? You've all the necessary skills and I think you'd do really well".

Now praise and this sort of positive encouragement had not really been much to the fore in my subdued educational experience, and I must admit that initially the idea seemed absolutely ludicrous. He went on:-

"You'd get all sorts of grants, tax rebate and a chance to carry on some of your part-time work to help you financially".

"Yes, but", I replied "I've two young children, a mortgage and the usual household expenses to think about. I don't honestly think it's feasible?"

"With your background, qualifications (HNC metallurgy), you could be a candidate for a two years only teacher training course".

Further prolonged discussions that evening gave me real food for thought, and I was further encouraged by my wife June suggesting that she too was ready for an appropriate local part-time job, that could be fitted around the childrens' school day. The following Monday evening, the same procedure took place but this time documentation, government booklets, local education pamphlets and several reading books were given to me to peruse – the seeds were sown then allowed to grow and bloom.

To my shame I cannot recall the name of this man who had radically changed my life without prompting. His shrewd observation, sensitivity, awareness and deep insight had spotted my potential; and he wasn't afraid to make a move on me – entirely for my benefit. He alone propelled me into full time education. Tragically, I understand that a few years later he lost his life in a boating accident. I never heard the details because by then we had left Sheffield to live in Leeds. What a waste.

At that time I also qualified as a part-time Further Education teacher, and began to attend many part-time or weekend courses to increase my subject area knowledge. I also began to write to colleges specifically to solicit a two- year course – we reckoned financially that for two years we could survive – although our belts would be very tight indeed.

The final straws, which broke the industrial camel's back, followed in quick succession. Firstly I achieved substantial pay increases for my staff, but because I was considered 'management' I was given a derisory 50p. Then I was passed over for a job I could have done very well, then asked to see to the welfare of the appointee and teach him the job! Thirdly I was called out on a hot May night to supervise the finishing of a huge forging that had to be completed and dispatched the following morning.

As I stood there in the midst of honest, bare-chested forgemen, earning by the way about three times my daily wage, I suddenly knew what St. Paul had experienced on the road to Damascus. I didn't give a toss whether this forging was done and dusted on time. It really didn't matter to me any more because I wanted to be with young people and do things, that shaped and influenced young minds. I wanted a people job. I turned on my heels and simply switched off, going through the motions with this company until I could hopefully leave in early September.

Several offers of a three year course emerged, even a one year course to teach Science, but there was no chance of this whatsoever. Happily at the eleventh hour in mid-August, an offer was extended by Huddersfield College to do a three-year course in two.

I knew my interview had gone well but the good news was tensely extracted from my sister-in-law, living in my home whilst we were holidaying in Wales.

She had been told to open any letters with a Huddersfield postmark, and she did this over the phone when I called her. She then painstakingly read the contents to me and the suspense was unbearable.

"Brenda, it's really important that you tell me if I've been offered a shortened course".

"Yes, you've definitely been accepted"

"I know that Brenda, but is it three years or two years they're offering, I know they're going to accept me, but it's the time span that is important ?"

Another long, mind-churning pause, then Brenda confirmed my two-year admission.

I finished off my industrial time, unashamedly giving the company nothing. They got what they deserved from me as I simply strolled through the last few days. Can I remind you of the book's foreword; Bill had been proved right yet again, there really was "nowt like wanting".

Thus college began at thirty-five years of age in 1971.

CHAPTER 5

College Days

I found college, and mixing with a totally new sort of clientele, stimulating, exciting and controversial, and have to confess that it radically changed my mind-set and life approach. Obviously, at 35, I was amongst the senior of the group and we were affectionately called matures – a term I believe still used today for any 21 year old or more being educated. When I arrived at Huddersfield I really hadn't a clue which age group I wanted to teach. I actually hadn't thought about it. I certainly had been busy over the last few weeks fending off the doubters; the teachers of my own children were the biggest culprits. My parents weren't convinced either, and there were others of whom I was more dismissive. These couldn't have accepted a challenge under any circumstances.

Anyway I settled for Secondary teaching, a very wise move, and also took Drama and Youth Counselling as my support subjects - even wiser moves. Throughout my college time I could never understand why fellow students found themselves besieged. I can honestly say that never during these two years – remember I'm no academic just a slogger – was I remotely stretched. I loved reading and English was, of course, my main study area. My wife would often say ,

"Haven't you got work to do tonight?"

"Well I've got to read 'The Outsider' I replied "and this Henry James' novel"

"Was that work"? you might well ask.

I will always believe that you can't teach people how to teach. It's either there to a sufficient or greater extent, or it isn't. We can learn to empathise, we can examine psychological approaches, we can learn tolerance, and compassion for those less fortunate, but we can't actually make anyone communicate effectively in front of a class of children

As a student and student teacher, when I came across a good practitioner, it literally made my neck hairs stand up. Passion, knowledge, control, discipline without being harsh or cruel, were the hallmarks of these people; and I learned so much as a student from watching and listening to them promote their skills.

My group were, in the main, a joy to be with, and 30 years on, I'm still in touch with some. They too taught me so much. I had few problems with the course work, but had time only for two six-week teaching practices. I still find it astonishing that I took a position at the city's second largest Comprehensive School with just twelve weeks teaching experience of which to boast.

My first teaching practice was at Rawthorpe, then a Secondary School teaching English and Drama. I was both astonished and appalled at the leadership I found there. Let's give for example the daily assembly routine:

1. School assembles, all standing up.
2. Head begins by announcing hymns.
3. Whether Christian, Atheist, Agnostic or Muslim, everyone must sing.

4. Fearsome individual fixing his eyes upon those of us not daring to sing including me the student teacher.
5. Head's daily announcement.
6. Head's prayers and talk of the value of love, tolerance and understanding.
7. Conclusion.
8. Head selects a number of pupils to stay behind whilst the remainder file out of the Hall.
9. Head walks off stage carrying a huge bible.
10. Head proceeds to bash on the head all those required to stay behind with self-same bible.

"You lad – weren't singing were you?" Bash!

"Don't... bash! ...come in here... bash! ...with the wrong attitude... bash!"

Every single selected student received identical treatment, and then for good measure, they all got another bash from behind before they left, bemused, stunned and not surprisingly wobbling a little from side to side.

They weren't the only ones stunned. What had changed since 1948 when I'd witnessed the Ecclesfield thrashing? What was I doing here disillusioned, and furthermore, with huge question marks hanging over the decisions I had made. I confessed all this at home that night but decided to see the six weeks through and take it from there.

The kids weren't that bad really. I enjoyed most of my time at this Secondary School and remember playing a newspaper English game with a huge leaving class of fifteen year olds. This was of course before the raising of the school leaving age. These pupils were affectionately known at that time as R.O.S.L.A. children. Most of these were very disaffected simply because they had to stay on at school for a further year. Half-way through the lesson,

I was approached by a tall, mature Asian lad who whispered in my ear:-

"Sir you are flying low" - I was nonplussed.

"Sir your flies!!"

I will never forget that – a touch of class in a fairly rough and rude school. He became a good mate and his maturity was astonishing.

I walked by the Head's office one day to see – yet again – one of the students I'd taught sitting outside.

"What're you doing here again then Fred?"

"Been caught smoking sir"

"How many times is that this week then Fred?"

"Three times sir"

"What happens in there then Fred?"

"I get four whacks of the cane sir"

"What for smoking?"

"Yep"

The cruel irony of all this was that man giving the punishment, with his own yellow nicotine stained hands, was a forty plus a day smoker!!

Unbelievable. Unacceptable.

My second teaching practice was a little more civilised with much more Drama involved, which I really loved. Incidentally both schools offered me a post when I had finished my two year course, but what none of us realised at the time was that I would be undergoing a third year in pursuit of an honours degree. Heavy stuff now for an 11+ failure.

A lovely circle was completed for me in 1993 when I – as a Headteacher – was asked to appraise the Head teacher – not the same one obviously – of the school where I had been a student teacher twenty years previously. The deputy I interviewed on this occasion, as part of the process, was the Drama teacher who had so carefully and patiently looked after me as I struggled successfully through my practice - another lovely Fred, another astonishing coincidence.

My two-year course drew to its conclusion. We had some undoubted hiccups, some altercations, and some political misgivings – there were far too many scruffy left-wingers around for me. I'd been brought up in a split conservative/labour household. When Mum and Dad walked arm in arm to vote on polling day, they knew for a fact they were just cancelling each other out (politics were that simple for them). I could well do however without the whingers and dissidents sometimes trying to dissuade me from what I sincerely believed to be right. I knew what I wanted to do, and I knew how I wanted to do it. (Incidentally, as I have already stated, some of the most vocal dissidents had been our own childrens' Junior and Infant school teachers in Sheffield).

I had few difficulties with lecturers, losing my cool and walking out on a lecture delivered with so much communist drivel interlaced with the lecture's main content, just the once. Once was enough to ensure there were no repeats. Similarly a students' union meeting, where the "brothers" and "comrades" routine blinded any positive objectives, was only attended the once.

I was approached one day by the college Vice Principal who suggested to me that I stay on at Huddersfield to do an Honours Degree in Education. This was right out of the blue and was not something actually on the agenda, or which had been budgeted for. After hasty talks with the bank and building society, who were absolutely fantastic, and realising that my previous industrial qualifications were now coming into play, I went on to reach the required entry level.

I looked back then on the three times a week, fifteen miles round' trips on my bicycle, arriving home after a twelve hour day of work and study. At last some reward for a punishing, demanding schedule. Inclement weather meant the nearest bus stop was a two miles or so walk to my home and arrival there sometimes after ten o'clock. Slogging days these might have been, but now there was the rewarding feel that they were leading to something vital.

So the 11+ failure at the age of thirty-eight was awarded a degree with honours at Leeds University in 1974 in front of proud parents and children. All I had to do now was find a September job, with the whole of the summer to find some work to reward the family with a two-week summer holiday in Cornwall.

My next chapter has to be included because it gave me some additional final perspectives of the 'real' world, before being somewhat cocooned in that vastly different educational environment.

Chapter 6

"If a Man Means Well"

I had several jobs in between my study terms and between the years of 1972 and 1974. These involved being a post-man, the driver of a large furniture van, a van loader for British Gas equipment, a Wimpey dumper driver, and the supervisor of a team of students working for Canada Dry, who at this time had a bottling plant in Leeds.

The latter was my final fling alongside industrial and business managers before University began, and involved the supervising of a bunch of students drawn from local Colleges and Universities. We worked the night shift alongside a regular but skeleton maintenance staff, and one overall boss drawn each week from the company's management team. The students themselves were mature and mostly very committed – Africans, East/West Europeans, Asians – a most cosmopolitan outfit.

I only had to sack one man in my eight week stint there, a character who decided to slip home, then slip back eight hours later, hoping we would think he was in the loo! Unfortunately for him, his mates weren't happy that he'd be paid just the same as them for skiving, and told me exactly where he would reappear in the morning. He virtually fell into my arms as he came over the fence, and his services were dispensed with immediately!

One night the bottling machines broke down and I was enthralled to see three Nigerian engineering students supporting the company's maintenance team to remedy the situation. Such was their quality that they didn't just sit back, as they so easily might have done, but got stuck in until the line was moving again.

One of the young managers on duty one week was called Richard – a total idiot if ever I saw one. He would come around to where the stackers of the crates of bottles were working – easily the most arduous of the tasks we had to do – and watch the lads steadily doing their level best.

"No Roy, look, this is the speed I want them to go at"

Then for five minutes he would go berserk while we all watched in open-mouthed amazement at the rapidly increasing height of cases. Then eyes popping, hair awry, sweat running down his face onto his immaculate white smock, he would stagger away to sit down.

"Richard, these lads have almost eight hours to do of this. Ever heard of the tortoise and the hare?"

He was rude and aggressive and a poor manager of people, and I had to step into a few confrontations and smooth many matters over. After a week however someone else took his place. This was indeed a Company Director; a calm, confident supportive man-manager who half-way through the night, at 2 o'clock in the morning actually, called me into his office for a whisky. I'd been here before!

We had a general talk on how the scheme – a unique one via Manpower services – was working and he expressed the fact that the company were delighted at the maximising of production during a long hot summer.

"Roy do you fancy a management job here?" was the next casual question that completely floored me.

I was trying to get away from all this; the hassle, the noise, the dirt. I was extremely flattered at the offer, especially when he mentioned the salary, a stupendous amount for an almost penniless student. Pause.

"Thanks, but no thanks Mr Sheridan. I do really want to teach. I really do want a degree"

"Well get yer degree lad and start with us next year"

"But I want to teach you see"

"Aagh, well it was worth a try, but while we're at it what's your opinion of Richard as a manager?"

Another huge pause here….

"Well… he's raw, inexperienced, naïve and in my humble opinion far too young for the job. But although at the moment he's about as useful to the company as a chocolate teapot, no doubt he will learn. Sadly I find no warmth in him. He definitely needs a management course."

Had I gone too far, had I jumped into a great hole from which it would be difficult to extricate myself? Mr Sheridan fixed me with a quizzical look and it was some moments before he spoke.

"Aye lad, that's exactly my opinion. We're sending him away to Bolton on a course to learn about managing people next Monday. Are you sure you won't come and work for us?"

Again I reflected on this out of the blue offer as I wandered from station to station in that industrial factory, watching these young student men of the future and wondering what life would offer to us once we were all qualified. The jobs of these men rotated each evening, but no matter which unsavoury job came their way in turn, there were few complaints, and some responsibilities were much easier than others.

I served as a postman for two successive Christmases in my local town of Garforth, enjoying the 6am. starts and the cycling involved. My friend's two young sons aged seven and nine asked me one day if they might accompany me. I responded in the affirmative thinking they'd never be up by 6am. anyway. However they were – waiting at the door for me on a bleak black December morning. Obviously the lads wanted to be participants, and to actually post the letters through the letter boxes, and the older one had few problems. Eventually we came to a location called 'The Oval', part of a council estate. Here the idea was that I'd go one way round and meet Sean, the younger and Simon the elder coming the other way round, as we delivered respectively. Sean had taken the odd numbers, Simon the even. I was impressed when Sean met me empty handed within seconds of us starting the street.

"You were sharp weren't you?"

"Oh I had a job getting them all in Uncle Roy, but I managed it" was his happy response.

"How do you mean…all?"

You've guessed it; he had put his whole bundle through the first letter-box on his side which he came across. Luckily, a light was on upstairs and so I knocked on the door, which was duly opened by the surprised owner.

"Please can I have my letters back?" I asked, totally embarrassed and feeling a complete idiot.

The owner complied with scarcely any expression of surprise, I don't think he actually took in what had happened.

The other 'between term' employment I enjoyed was working with a team of Irishmen for Wimpey house builders. I was the dumper truck driver and never have I laughed so much at work before or since. Watching them putting curb stones in the wrong way round and puzzling about the difficulties, shrieking in fear when a large water hose which, when switched on, bulged unexpectedly, and then jettisoned a full mouse's nest across the road, or when one of them asked to have a little go on my dumper and went straight through a garage door. John Bowland a lovely warm Irish foreman who had to control his very mentally limited team used to dismiss all the mishaps and eccentricities with a beautifully turned out phrase

"Roy me boy, so long as a man means well". If John said this once then he said it to himself and others twenty times a day.

He even consoled me with the words when I failed to secure my dumper bucket after cleaning out all the drains. The full load spewed across a main road and had to be re-shovelled and hosed down.

The gang, against all the rules, used to eat their packed lunches upstairs in the only finished house which was also used for prospective buyers to view. Every lunchtime, I would pick up all the wrappings and sometimes fish and chip papers until in the end I just got fed up. Sure enough the site manager came along one afternoon with a customer and stumbled across the mess. John got a real rollicking.

"John you've been in that house when you'd no business to haven't you? Well you've no f...... reason to and it's not to be messed up by a mucky lot of b...... like you!"

Later in the afternoon John turned to me and said,

"Sure Roy me boy, how on earth did he know we'd been upstairs, we kept well away from the window". He meant it too.

A happy hot summer. Good money in my pocket. Brown as a berry. I only wore boots, socks and shorts for weeks on end. When I left I was able to collect equipment such as shovels, picks, a wooden sawhorse and bags of cement from that site. These were all due to be buried as the work ended, or so I was informed. Still using some of these tools today reminds me of these final few weeks in working mode before education, finally and fully, enveloped me.

But again I'd learned so much about people, their strengths, their failings, their needs, and their expectations. It was all, so important in the long run, as I moved into a whole new and exciting life.

Chapter 7

Comprehensively Enjoyed

I went for two formal interviews in that spring of 1974. The first, to a school in Goole, where the outcome was indeterminate. Was I supposed to ring them, or they me – I never found out which? Goole was too far away in any event.

I also went to a girls' prison in Wakefield but there were too many locked doors to negotiate. The Prison Head was a lovely woman who showed me their latest success story in the Daily Mirror, where a former beautiful inmate had just been acknowledged as one of the country's leading Alsation breeders. She had risen to these dizzy heights via page 3 stardom in the Sun newspapers.

I think it was sensed, rather than determined, that I hadn't actually the stomach or the security to deal with a hardened class of female juvenile criminals. Thus noble intentions to serve those less fortunate and disadvantaged fell at the first hurdle. Better, I thought, to try and prevent them getting into this predicament in the first place. I believe I argued this to both appease my conscience, and to save face.

Absolutely by chance, a job landed in my lap. In these days of equal opportunity and rigid rules of educational employment, it simply wouldn't have happened, even though teacher shortages now do mean some short cuts and some relaxation of educational bureaucracy.

I'd been doing some evening drama classes and I approached the Head of this particular evening institution, who also worked at the nearby Garforth Comprehensive School, to determine if I might undertake some B. Ed. English work there? This in turn led to me being noticed by a beautiful English teacher called Corinne Corcoran whose beauty was matched by her exquisite teaching skills. I had also been seen, unknowingly, by the Head and Deputies of the School. Incidentally Corinne was to die at the tender age of 26 and her loss to the teaching profession was profound.

One morning, wearing gardening jeans and an old shirt and whilst out walking the dog, I literally popped into the school to collect some English work to mark from one of my groups there. A deputy came out of his office.

"Mr Norcliffe isn't it? Can you spare a minute to talk to Mr Scott (The Headteacher) and myself?"

Oh dear – had someone complained about me? Trying to avoid the issue, I responded.

"Sorry I've got the dog here, it's a bit difficult."

"She'll be alright, just tie her to that bench. We won't be long."

Mystified, I was led into the Head's office and without much ado was complimented by the Head and Deputy on my style and relationships with the kids.

"Would you like a job in the English Department here?"

"Pardon?" – question repeated.

"Yes, I think I would," much stammering "but both my kids are in the school, isn't that a problem?"

"Not really, you'll never teach them and we're so big – 1800 students incidentally – you're not always certain even to see them around the place."

I couldn't believe my good fortune. Again someone up there was putting me into the right place at the right time. I was overjoyed. The School had a fine reputation and my family, perhaps understandably with mixed reactions from the kids, were generally overjoyed.

So in September 1974 I began teaching at Garforth Comprehensive School – a humble English teacher with a keen interest in Educational Drama. Not necessarily play or theatre based, but Drama, which could be used as role play for explaining issues, developing confidence and awareness. or simply helping other curriculum areas such as History and R.E. to become more meaningful and more exciting. My starting salary was terribly low but the potential for more was patently obvious.

I loved every minute finding it stimulating, exciting, rewarding, and often hilarious. The weeks simply flew by. Just before my first half-term holiday in October I received a note to make an appointment with the Head teacher. Help!

In industry when a call came from above it was inevitably to deliver a blistering warning, a rollicking for perceived inadequacies or a dressing down of some sorts. What had I done wrong in a mere seven weeks? What dreadful mistake merited my being called to order? Rack my brains as I could, I had no idea of the reason for this meeting.

Thus at 38 years of age I experienced my first taste of man-management at its best; as I nervously eased myself into a comfortable chair to talk to a man who became a total inspiration to me during the two and a half years he and I were together at Garforth. Edwin Scott began.

"Roy, what are your plans and thoughts for the future in teaching?"

Thoughts, plans - I'd not given any consideration whatsoever to the future. I stumbled and stuttered a very unconvincing response.

"Not sure Edwin, why?"

You see, I was still expecting a rebuke. Industry had instilled into me into this sort of expectation. (Was Edwin about to say "Future, you haven't got one here.")

"What sort of salary do you envisage in say four years time Roy?"

Again, I must have been embarrassingly lost for words. Damn it, I'd only been in teaching seven weeks. I'd all on to survive worrying about the immediate future, never mind the more distant one. I'd no idea anyway what was paid above a Scale 1.

Thankfully the farce ended – I hadn't done too well so far – with hesitant, ill at ease responses until Edwin explained:

"You see we've been watching you as you go about your work. We like your attitude, admire your teaching skills, are delighted with the way you respond to young people and allow them to engage with you. We think you were born to this profession."

As the saying goes I was gob-smacked! Never in my life had I been party to such praise and recognition of my skills. Skills I was only just beginning to realise I had anyway.

Edwin continued.

"Actually I want you here with me at Garforth in four years time – by which time you'll be a formidable Head of Year – and so the plaudits went on.

I left the office and can't remember walking home. I was on cloud nine because someone I totally respected had taken the time and the trouble to compliment me. No pay rise, no job promotion but what I'd experienced was paradoxically just as rewarding, if not more so.

Within fifteen months I had been promoted to Head of Drama and allowed access to the sort of decision making and visionary thinking I'd always dreamt about. My first production at Garforth was the musical 'Oliver'. The Heads of Music, Needlework (Art and Fabric, as it is called now, but needlework in 1976!) discussed my ideas and plans for a massive whole school venture, and our combined enthusiasms harboured nothing but promise of an exciting project.

So in 1976, the vision was actually conceived, apart from one minor tantrum from Dave Hinkley, a wonderful and inspirational music teacher who, after a bad rehearsal, responded to me by saying

"How the f...... hell, you f...... persuaded me to do the f...... show I'll never know. We're not up to it."

Dave sought perfection you see and he always got it. In fact he achieved almost perfection for production after production in the late 1970s and later for other Heads of Drama. His relationship with the kids and his magnificent patience with youngsters was legendary.

He even forgave my son who at the age of thirteen and fooling about in class, as was his wont actually fell out of the ground floor music room window. Good job it wasn't today as the music room is now on the second floor! (These however were the only blips I can recall in the whole three months of production preparation).

Edwin Scott again showed his magnificent humanity and humility in another altogether fraught situation for me. Late into rehearsals the upper sixth student playing Fagin bowed to parental pressure and backed out of the show. Resigned to playing the role myself I received a note to see Edwin as soon as I could.

All my initial awkwardness had gone when confronted by this man but I was still unsure of what he wanted me for. But in any event he was always great to talk to and I always enjoyed chewing matters over with him.

"Roy, I understand you have lost your Fagin for 'Oliver?'"

"Correct Edwin but I'll play him myself. A challenge, but there's not much alternative I'm afraid."

"Roy, can I play him please?"

Here he was, the great man himself, actually begging me for the part!

I was absolutely stunned yet again. Edwin at times had a really bad stutter, but in public appearances this disappeared but I'd no idea whether he could act/sing/dance at all. He was the Head teacher of the City's second largest Comprehensive School for heaven's sake!

Could he sing, could he act, could he dance? Couldn't he just – all three with total conviction and superb panache. He stepped

There's Nowt Like Wanting

into rehearsals, the kids loved him and he moved the whole affair up by several gears and also became pure box office. 'The All Singing Head'. Full houses for six nights and two afternoons with over one hundred people having to be turned away on the Saturday night. The show was pure magic and perhaps the most rewarding thing of my life – and remember I'd acted and directed in many shows before then, at all sorts of levels.

Perhaps equally rewarding were the number of friends and parents who stopped me in the street to say that it was perhaps, from a theatrical point of view, the most impressive thing to ever hit Garforth. Praise indeed.

The Head also managed to free children from other lessons during the penultimate week of the production, naturally to the accompaniment of moans and groans from a few – just a few staff. Other teachers failed to see or appreciate my 'three nights a week' working until six o'clock to prepare the work. One such grumbler, a science teacher – he lives near me so I'd better withhold names – was brought by Edwin into the hall. Edwin reported the discussion as follows.

"Denis came into my office bemoaning the fact that you had several of his Biology pupils in the main hall rehearsing."

"Oh dear," I replied.

"Not to worry Roy," Edwin cheerfully responded, "I took him into the hall and said the day you can cope with over 150 pupils working in such a civilised and often unsupervised manner but yet committed to the cause is the day I'll refuse Roy permission to rehearse." (This was certainly never going to happen).

Rather than carping wouldn't it have been terrific if a Scientist could have acknowledged and appreciated the massive amount of learning and team-work being engendered that particular day.

Both Edwin and Laurie Lowton who succeeded him in 1976 were totally supportive in all I did in the world of Drama, backing every move I made as Drama became a CSE, GCSE and A Level subject on the school curriculum. Today the centre stands at the pinnacle of the Arts and is recognised as a School of excellence in Performing Arts. It's good to know that I was its initiator and visionary almost thirty years ago. Happily I return there to this very day as an A Level Drama and Theatre Studies examiner.

I have mentioned the numerous musical productions in my time at Garforth, but tragedy surrounded the 1980 production of 'The Sound Of Music'.

I decided that a talented year ten student would play Maria. Jane was an excellent dancer and singer, and a very capable actress, and I was acutely aware this was the first time I had selected someone for a lead part below years eleven to thirteen.

Her Mum, Elsie, who worked in the school library, stood beside me one evening during dress-rehearsal week.

"I'm not sure she's ready for the heavy responsibility yet Roy" she worried.

"Trust me, Elsie" I replied. "You've seen her without an audience in rehearsal, just watch her respond to a full house".

Jane was superb, and Elsie followed every breath-taking minute with avid enthusiasm. She was particularly moved at seeing her youngest daughter in a wedding dress.

One week later, Elsie and her husband, Alan, lost their lives in the 1980 Tenerife Air Disaster – a terrible time for us all.

Another fond memory of the School is a literary weekend in the Yorkshire Dales and this was led by Edwin Scott himself. We looked at comedy in literature, which meant at one point the Head receiving a custard pie in the face. Again it was unbelievable the furore this caused back at school. What did staff really expect their Head teacher to be and do? Edwin refused to fit staff Head teacher expectations but his charisma was absolutely terrific. My six and a half years at Garforth were magnificent I had learned so much. When I was asked to become a Head of Year in 1978 I was delighted to accept. To other staff however I was still a rookie, and I was actually omitted from several Christmas card lists that year!

I had always believed that teachers liked – at the very least – children and was astounded to discover that many didn't do so. I remember one language teacher – another complainant at losing children from her lessons for the School Production – looking out of the staff room at the Easter early leavers.

"Thank God to see the back of those swine," was her riposte.

I looked at her in astonishment, what a remark to make in public. Now was a good time to remind her of her anti-production attitude.

"By the way thanks for being very negative about my production. It's a good job I didn't take that same stance when you took some of my kids to France on that exchange trip."

Education in school is not, and never will be, being in the same classroom day after day. Other experiences matter – matter deeply – and thank God the pattern now, despite the depressing doom and gloom of the dismal Health and Safety merchants, is for even more 'value added' experiences. These alternative experiences have, I believe, a miniscule effect on an individual's traditional academic learning.

Presenting 'My Fair Lady' in 1977 a superb colleague and friend to this day, Dave Flaherty played Professor Higgins. When it came to the section where Eliza has to pronounce her consonants via the candle flame we discovered that some Sixth form wag (Sixth form under their wonderfully eccentric Head, Peter Johnson, always supplied stage management) had so doctored the candle that it wouldn't light. After what seemed an eternity Dave managed it but at the end of the show wanted blood! The air was blue and word was sent down the line that both Dave and myself wanted the same blood. We didn't see the culprit, night or day, for a week, such was his fear of us. Putting it into perspective took time but we will never forget our consternation at that moment. Dave on stage left, literally a few inches from me in the wings, nearly suffered apoplexy. I kept repeating

"Leave the bloody thing, pretend it's lit" which didn't exactly go down well, especially within earshot of the children. Dave's extra expletives at curtain call raised a few eyebrows even further.

There were two particular Heads of Year at this wonderful establishment with respective and contrasting styles. Their different management skills of pupils and staff had equally stimulating results. I confess that I adopted and integrated both their philosophies and beliefs. I added these to the values that I already had for myself. Both of these men progressed in the field of education to very high levels – again this was not surprising.

Whilst my curriculum duties were a major part of my responsibilities at Garforth, my pastoral duties demanded equal attention. As Head of Year, I was responsible for approximately 330 young people, and the vast majority managed to conduct themselves properly in accordance with learning and disciplinary requirements.

However, there had to be a few exceptions, and Derek was to be the single most difficult pupil during my time at Garforth.

Derek came to us from a Special School, and it had been decided that for his final two years of mandatory education, he would be placed in a Mainstream School.

After meeting him one day, I took his file home, and it made horrendous reading. Both parents and stepparents had died, and Derek had witnessed his sister abort her child after falling down her cellar steps. Furthermore, he was deaf and had a severe speech defect. However, Derek was a battler, and I personally was determined to give him as much time, consideration, and care as I could. This often took me into direct conflict with my own management team but I knew that Education Welfare were very much with me. Several times his school place was threatened as he blew his very short fuse.

I negotiated a special timetable for Derek, giving him both the curriculum-study areas and sympathetic caring teachers, which I considered appropriate. They call it Flexible Learning these days. I called it common sense.

Derek had a part in our production of 'Oh What A Lovely War', and had just one line, something like "Stop sergeant or I'll have to ------". It was a chorus line but try as he might, Derek could only stammer "Ssssssss" up to the first night.

The rest of the cast were really supportive of him, willing the line to come out of his mouth, but quite certain it wouldn't. There was always a deathly hush before his line, but inevitably, our hopes were dashed. I was determined to leave the line in anyway knowing that the cast were able to cover up the situation.

Come first night, the usual hush but out came the line as clear as a bell. The spontaneous happy reaction of those on stage somewhat puzzled the audience, but for each and every performance after that, Derek rose to the challenge.

He used to call and see us for quite a while after leaving school, but where he is now, I'm afraid I have no idea. It was, however, one of the most significant challenges and happy outcomes of my whole career- the sort of success which made teaching so rewarding.

Without being romantic the six and a half years at Garforth were simply the best – better than all the rest as Tina Turner would say. We were allowed to do things in the 1970's that can't happen today. Weekends away with pupils, activity days, walking the Three Peaks, living on uninhabited Hebridean Islands et al. For example one early spring evening, nine of us took off after school to Cirencester where a friend of mine ran a Cotswold pub and whose inebriates were keen sportsmen and women. A challenge was issued to our school, and nine of us represented Garforth.

Finishing an English standardisation meeting chaired by our own Head of English, but involving several local Comprehensive schools, four of the nine sat at the back ready for early Friday night take off down the M1. Frequent pointing to our wristwatches, gesticulations and mouthed 'Come on Alan', eventually reaped reward and we scuttled out, on our way South.

At 7.30pm darts, skittles, dominoes and cribbage commenced. At 10.30pm we joined Jean our hostess, and friends, at the Ladies annual darts' dance at the Cirencester Town Hall. At 1.00am in the morning most bedded down in sleeping bags on the skittle alley floor. I was fortunate as their personal friend to have the benefit of a proper bed. Jean cooked a full fry up breakfast for us all, and then we competed in a five a side football match in the Abbey Gardens, followed by squash and swimming after lunch. After quick goodbyes, we set off North for a Chinese meal with wives and girlfriends which concluded a crazy thirty two hours!. My endearing memory is of Flaherty – not much of a footballer

- scuffling in the rhododendron bushes at the Abbey for a loose ball. Bush, opponent and Flaherty emerged in that order, but Dave had the ball.

Crazy days as I said but goodness how these guys could play and teach way ahead of any teaching staff I ever encountered in later days. Richly talented and gifted people! The achievements of so many Garforth students was extraordinary, and so many reached great heights.

In 1976 my teaching world was turned upside down, when Edwin Scott the Head Teacher was offered and accepted an H.M.I. post. At the time I was chair of the staff committee, so many of his farewell arrangements were left to me. Paradoxically I was asked to direct a Drama Teachers' Course by the Leeds Education Services and as a consequence missed the actual presentation day.

He was replaced by an entirely different species. Toughened in an inner city school, the new Head brought inner-city management styles to a leafy lane Comprehensive. Some new ideas never got off the ground but to be fair, others were necessary and were right and proper changes. However the two contrasting styles gave me something to think about. Encouragement and the trust that we Heads of Year would get on with it, versus rule by fear.

I learned so much from both men and Laurie was actually the one who offered me the Head of Year post and then saw off the authority who insisted it be advertised and candidates interviewed. Equal opportunity was beginning to raise its head – never mind the fact that you had every faith and confidence in an individual and didn't need to go through the rigmarole! I faced this dilemma years after as a Headteacher myself when the authority (KIRKLEES) made me advertise for posts when I already had temporary teachers proving themselves day after day in a tough school. My heart went out to those unfortunates I had to interview knowing that my decision had already been made. I think they too, often knew the score and the 'internal candidate syndrome'.

However I believe I picked up the best from both my Head teacher bosses and still developed my individual management style which had a modicum of success.

Much as I loved my work as Head of Year and Head of School and Community Drama, I began to feel the need to progress. I had been at Garforth just over six years now, was forty four years of age, and with time running out if I was to run my own school by the age of fifty.

A number of Deputy Head applications came to very little (references taken up here and there) until in October 1980 I landed – at my first interview- a Deputy post in a South Leeds School. This had once been an outstanding working class Grammar School but was to be a massively different experience from my last six years at Garforth.

My final assembly before the whole school of some sixteen hundred pupils was memorable in one particular instance; a happening which did so much for my belief in myself – even if this was already becoming considerable anyway.

After usual staff management plaudits all the kids in my numerous drama groups and some members of my year group spontaneously rose to their feet to sing 'for he's a jolly good fellow!' Staff implored them to sit down and shut up but they would have none of it until they'd done. This had never happened before and quite frankly Senior Management, and some staff, found it threatening, but at a gesture from me, all sixty or so of them settled down without a murmur. Terrific stuff this, thinking

There's Nowt Like Wanting

for themselves – not always encouraged in some educational establishments!

So in December 1980 after six years and one term only in teaching I faced the daunting prospect of life at a tough inner-city school where morale was low and achievement was limited. Had I learned sufficient at Garforth to make an impact here? Why was I giving up a post where I was developing myself and clearly developing both students and some colleagues and above all where I was incredibly self-fulfilled? Questions, questions but I had to suck it and see.

It would however, be a particular shame to depart from this time of my career without mentioning two Summer Schools, which I directed at the behest of Leeds Authority, in the early 1980's.

The first was for 'Gifted' children, the second one, a year later, for 'Disadvantaged and Educationally Limited young people' – a massive contrast.

'Gifted'! What an unfortunate title we were to foolishly place on this week-long residential course. The young people on board were however, extradordinarly bright and hand picked from both Junior and Secondary schools. The six staff, too, were amongst the Authority's 'cream'; even so keeping abreast of the childrens' voracious appetites for learning and knowledge, was demanding and exhausting for us all.

Politically, the course was a mine-field, and often standing in the meal-time queues, other older students on campus would 'rib' our children by saying such things as:

"Are you a gifted kid then?" or

"What's it like to be gifted like you, wish I was?"

Usually this was said in 'fun', but point taken, and because the course was residential, there was constant exposure. The youngsters themselves however, took it all in their stride, and with great good humour.

Similarly, the course for the educationally limited children meant hand picked staff of different but still oustanding skills. The fact that two of these served on both courses, is testament to their great ability. The course was held at a Special School, on the banks of the River Wharfe, near Harrogate, and presented lots of opportunities for out-door activity and practically biased lessons.

Flaherty decided that one night we would prepare a 'Trout and Chicken Bar-b-que' to parents and friends. It was my job to collect the fish and game, and after I had collected the trout, I called at a Chicken Farm on my way back to base. Imagine my surprise and consternation when these were given to me very much alive!

"Er, I think the kids are going to dress them", I said, "but killing them I think not". Visions of twenty or so children chasing chickens around the estate before mutilating them beyond recognition came to mind, and seeing my indecision, the farmer immediately rang their necks and threw them into my vehicle – still convulsing.

The children did indeed dress and cook both chickens and fish to tasty perfection, and after a series of games, including 'welly throwing', their preparations were much appreciated by us all.

I recall that were were visited by an HMI, and he first introduced himself to me as I was stood on a toilet, manfully trying to clean it with a huge toilet cleaner, after it had been blocked by a particular piece of nastiness.

We came through this inspection,despite being haunted by the Special School's Headteacher who lived just across the road, and who seemingly couldn't keep away. The man could not mind his own business and was a surly, unsupportive and quite dislikeable person, who obviously resented our prescence in his school. He could have been much more to us if he had so chosen.

The challenges of both these courses were obviously immense and a significant benefit to me in terms of both personal and professional development.

Chapter 8

A Change Is Not As Good As A Rest

Cockburn High School had been Cockburn Grammar School and had turned into a Comprehensive some three or four years earlier. Whilst I had little regret at the demise of some of these over-rated institutions, Cockburn had abandoned many of the standards which had given them real kudos. Management unforgivingly allowed themselves to think that going comprehensive meant liberalism, and an abandonment of the beliefs and standards that had made them centres of excellence.

The fact was that many of the staff found themselves unable, ill equipped, ill trained and totally unaware that they now had to try and teach often unmotivated and failing young people. It was to my mind criminal that no guidance, support or understanding of the cataclysmic changes coming their way had been offered by Leeds Education Authority in the mid 1970's. Let's analyse some of these:-

1. Why abandon an excellent uniform policy – those chocolate blazers, jumpers and ties were city famous – and allow Tetley bitter beer tee-shirts, and similar sloganed shirts, bovver boots etc. to be the new school uniform? Worst of all in those early year students in the old uniform were at war with the

'dress as you want' brigade. Unnecessary internal strife over appearances exacerbated numerous other issues, particularly for those Grammar School teachers untrained and unsuited to teach an intake which was now skewed distinctly downwards. Kowtowing to mediocrity was the general norm at the school.

2. Entrances and exits to the building were still proclaiming 'girls' and 'boys', the building being built in Victorian times, but something of an apology in terms of high ceilings, high windows and a severe design. Paradoxically the plans I believe were exhibited at the Albert museum, the principal highlight being its ducted heating system with each ducted vent leading into a classroom. A maze of vents in fact which were to eventually lead to the school's demise. Read on.

3. Pupils couldn't use the main front entrance at all – this being guarded and patrolled by staff – what a waste of man/woman power.

4. Assemblies! Here the young people were expected to sit on a dusty hall floor to try and pay attention to the daily rituals of notices, and other matters. I have no argument with assemblies starting each day on a note of togetherness, but let the other side at least be dignified, and comfortable. Eventually my suggestion that each pupil carry their own chair to and from assembly was acted upon. Simple or not?

5. Attendance. I couldn't believe my eyes and ears to be informed that it was my job each evening to take every register home and check absences for the whole school. What were the form tutors' pastoral duties I wondered – learning very quickly that they were largely non-existent. Therefore coming from a much bigger school that prided itself on its pastoral and disciplinary ethos I quickly realised I had a lot to do. Where to begin wasn't hard – registers!

It is important to inform the reader here that one of my rivals for this Deputy Headship was a popular internal candidate. Those of you who are familiar with insiders bidding for promotion recognise that these are, more often than not, popular with the general staff. Thus the feeling of sympathy for the failed internal candidate often heightens the hostility towards the successful outsider. I was in such a situation, especially with my revolutionary approach to running a successful school. I was generally considered as some sort of alien, even more so when I let it be known that I wasn't here to stay and had real ambition to Head my own school - certainly within five years and before I reached fifty years of age.

I very quickly realised that my predecessor, Mr Brown - how often were his saint-like qualities referred to – literally carried his staff with respect to the monitoring of pupils' progress, lateness, attendance and their general well being. Imagine each night recording every lateness and absence (almost 700 pupils). In the rich days of Grammar School gentleness maybe, but now it was yet another crazy carry over. The first thing therefore was to raise the awareness, credibility and responsibility of form tutors and not surprisingly they responded marvellously. They wanted class ownership welcomed form tutor time of a social and pastoral nature, and then worked naturally through Heads of Year, then myself on the major issues.

'But Mr Brown…..' gradually faded away.

Access to the building was also discussed and with three multi-sex entrances the need for guard duty and worry patrol was extinguished, literally overnight. I suppose that the immediate adjacent chapel and memorial to our former fallen ex-pupils was a shrine that had to be respected, and its proximity to the front entrance was a consideration. However never in my time at Cockburn was there ever any hint of abuse or desecration. We trusted the pupils and these rough, tough, inner city kids didn't let us down, and responded superbly.

Assemblies were easy too. Because the hall lacked plastic chairs we asked every pupil to carry and return their own chair to and from their classroom. Why another two hundred or so couldn't have been purchased to stay stacked up in the main hall was not a solution which received much sympathy. With the pupils seated properly the assemblies then became a much brighter, meaningful and less fidgety, moaning, groaning affair.

Getting the pupils into appropriate wear took a little longer. Surprise, surprise, their choice of school jumper was brown and their ties very closely resembled the old Grammar School ones.

Once these young people were smartly attired and with a sense of belonging, of real ownership and pride, you could feel the spirit lift amongst these youngsters of deprived South Leeds. From being a 1950's time warp it approached the 1980's in much better fettle.

The Headteacher was a quiet, gentle man, outstanding with finance budgets and administration but a little guarded in terms of relationships and management style. Timetabling generally, substitution for absent teachers, and staffing the examinations were admittedly a nightmare for me. Staff there were wonderful at letting you set up a system which might have one teacher in two different places at the same time. They then let you know WITH GREAT DELIGHT at the eleventh hour of your error! My writing of staffs' initials I must confess were not always clear either. I blew my top however just the once, when in doing the daily substitute list, there appeared 'smart arse' comments on the sheets and the moaners were waiting to pounce on my errors.

"Just go and do the f...... job" I instructed one such prat.

I remember too one night after school dealing with a miscreant, smoothing down an aggressive parent, and being a few minutes late for a staff meeting.

As I arrived, some moans and groans ensued from one particular teacher.

"Put a brush up my arse and I'll sweep the floor if you like Marjorie!"

"What, what did he say?" asked the English teacher in question.

My steelworks language (grossly modified) did have its value.

One of my biggest allies was Bill White – cynical unsmiling but a terrific professional, Bill teaches my Grandchildren now and it was he who spoke at my leaving Cockburn in 1986. I'll never forget his final tribute when he said that I was a man that people loved working for! A rare tribute from a man I greatly admired for so many outstanding qualities, and someone from whom I learned so much about inner-city educational deprivation, poverty and paucity of resources. Can I let you see Bill's parting shot, which he read out to staff on my final day at Cockburn.

To W. White

Head of Year

Cockburn High School

Leeds 11

TO BE GALLERY

LONDON

WC1

JULY 20TH 1986

Dear Mr White,

Thank you for your submission of the Roy Norcliffe work 'Substitution Timetable' for our forthcoming Impressionist Art Exhibition to be held early in 1983.

Whilst we are all very excited we feel it would be more appropriately placed elsewhere. You see the Impressionist school of painters consist of those artists who are well aware of what they are painting but choose not to represent their subjects in a purely factual way. It is patently obvious to us that Roy Norcliffe has never seen a substitution timetable let alone study the form it should take.

However as I mentioned earlier we can certainly use this piece of work with its bold strokes and unintelligible hieroglyphics in our ' to be held' exhibition on Primitive Painters.

We would also like to meet and talk with the artist before the event. I assume he has powers of speech.

Yours sincerely

Director

One day Bill came into my office and said.

"Roy, I'm sure there's a dog in the boss's office. I've heard it." The Head's office was just across the corridor, his dog we knew was a lovely little Sealyham Terrier.

"No Bill, can't be" but then we heard a low growl.

We both in turn bent down and peered through the keyhole. Sure enough there was the boss's tiny dog sat at his desk! We continued to peer in and wind up his dog, failing to notice the boss creeping silently up behind us.

"Alright chaps, everything ok?"

Caught in the act!

The Head was good at fixing door hinges, glazing, stopping leaking pipes and often did this rather than call upon in my opinion a very idle caretaker! One day as I approached him whilst he was fixing a door, a boy was flung out of the classroom by an irate teacher. He crashed into the wall opposite and fell into a crumpled heap. Neil carried on fixing the door, gathered his tools and stepped over the heap on the corridor floor with nary a word to anyone, and without a backward glance (I could never do that). The mopping up of pupil and staff was done of course by yours truly.

A tough school and often-tough times but another boost came with the appointment of my good friend, Colin, as fellow Deputy. Colin is still there now but as the Headteacher, and from being the 'Cinderella' school of notorious South Leeds, it now sets the benchmark. Together Colin and I had the vision and more importantly the philosophy and practical know-how to get important things through.

Another memory of the Head's attention to administration detail was when a visitor from Canada – a pupil of the 1940s – came and asked if she might have her leaving exam reports and her end of school results. She'd never collected them and wanted to prove to her newly qualified family that she had indeed done quite well at school. It took Neil literally five minutes or so in the basement to find these documents of forty years previous. Remarkable! We examined them together, marks for things like deportment, reading and poetry skills, and also marks for attitude to others. We could certainly do with some of these today. The visit made real news in the local press and was good publicity for the school.

I've mentioned these hot air ducts reminiscent of Charles Dickens 'Water Babies' chimney sweep scenes where a workman's voice from below would clearly carry through the whole school – and often did – to the clear embarrassment of the teachers and the delight of the pupils, particularly at some of the choice invectives used.

Well one day in late 1984 it was discovered that these famous ducts were actually lined with asbestos and little piles of dust all over the cellar floors suggested that, after over one hundred years, the asbestos was crumbling. Immediate school closure. Some classes were moved to the new sixth form building, and only myself, donned in a white spaceman's suit was allowed back in to rescue the livestock. A very leisurely two or three weeks ensued before the Christmas holidays.

Top level Leeds Authority discussions eventually led to the whole school being bussed to another site across the city (this building had already been earmarked for knock down). However it was about eight miles away on the outskirts of the city surrounded by green fields and woodland. What a marvellous change from the Cockburn site where it had taken a good ten-minute walk to get to the playing fields.

I had mixed feelings about transporting around six hundred pupils on a fleet of buses from their home environment and then bringing them back at the end of each day. I developed another talent, that of bus inspector, it being my job to be on the last bus up to school and first one away, so as to supervise the safe arrival of everyone at the end of the school day.

At that time education was in turmoil. Industrial action meant no after-school teachers' meeting, no parents' evenings etc. etc. However our personal situation meant that these couldn't happen anyway not with half the staff riding shot gun, leaving the other half to either stay or go home by car. This arrangement was done on a week on week off basis but I was always 'on' which meant early go home finishes and short working days. I can't remember what we did for period eight, or maybe we shortened down every period, but whatever we managed, every child was back in Leeds by 3.30pm each day, our normal finishing time.

I quite enjoyed this period, which for me lasted over two terms, before I left and for fellow staff, another half-term. But in between times we attended lots of public meetings about the fate of Cockburn the 'famous' old school. Apparently the cost of removing all the asbestos and making it safe together with all the other front line maintenance so badly needed after years of dire neglect made the total prohibitive.

I really sounded off at one large public meeting saying that the children deserved a more modern purpose built school, adjacent playing fields and real facilities. I think that I shocked a few people when I stated that my own working office was lit by a tiny high up window which was never cleaned and that I had to have the electric light on all day. (I didn't tell them of the heavy cane I'd discovered which was buried in a cupboard but which was used to inflict corporal punishment in by-gone years which further depressed that awful office). Instead I spoke of my new outlook of sunshine, sunsets, children playing games on the field, and of a background of valleys, fields and woods. They certainly began to think about things as I became quite passionate.

Well eventually Cockburn was knocked down, the temporary school in West Leeds was also knocked down and Cockburn pupils moved back to South Leeds to another establishment on a green belt site initially earmarked for demolition. This was ultimately given a two million pound face-lift and all the quality that could be afforded. Good on you Leeds.

Despite being involved in the exciting new developments I had also landed – at only my second attempt, a Headship in nearby Kirklees at a Huddersfield School. Amazingly, I just failed to land a Headship on my own stamping ground at Sheffield, but it was equally amazing that I was going back to my old training ground. I landed the post in March and unavoidably half my mind was on Deighton Community School, and a much more relaxed half in Cockburn.

I genuinely felt that my five and a half years had seen me make something of an impact even though two educational sites were no longer standing shortly afterwards! Two last anecdotes prevail in my memory, and must be told.

Soon after my appointment a very sophisticated and superior female Leeds adviser\came to see me. Immediately her attitude and tone got my back up. At Garforth I'd been very used to sympathetic and supportive advisers.

There was a lot of meaningless conversation of a very mundane nature before she said to me:

"I don't know how you managed to become a Deputy Head teacher in only six years" she said.

I paused before deliberately replying, as succinctly as possible.

"Because I'm bloody good!" – end of conversation.

A young man of previous good conduct was brought to me for calling the music teacher (Simon) a 'wanker'.

The lad was due to leave in a few weeks and his file was 'clean', therefore he was kept in isolation and sent home with a letter. Mum came to see me and he apologised in writing to the music teacher and after three days he returned to school. Pretty standard stuff. Remember the lad had not ever been a problem in his three years of schooling. I was therefore astonished to be confronted by the music teacher to complain that I hadn't been strong enough!

I pinned the unfortunate young teacher to the wall and said,

"Simon, who did he actually call a wanker?"

"Well…. me….." he stammered.

"Well what have you done about it Simon, and how will you now address the matter?" I walked away without waiting for a response. Later, coming to think about it, I knew the lad was right. He was a plonker!

However, I had achieved my ambition. The 11+ failure had reached the dizzy height of Headship at 49 years of age. At 50 my roller coaster Headship of Deighton High School and Community Education Centre commenced.

When I decided to go into teaching in 1971 the farthest thought in my mind was a Headship. How could an 11+ failure possibly Head a school – and a comprehensive school, never?

It didn't take me very long I can tell you to realise that the teaching competition – except for one or two exceptional cases – was not frightening. The skills I had and were developing by the day seemed considerably in front of the majority. Whilst at Garforth it became blindingly clear to me that I could make it to the top. In 1986 I did, bang on cue at the age of 50.

CHAPTER 9

Deighton Incorporated

I began this phase of my educational career believing that I would continue to reign for the next 15 years, or so and then move on into retirement. After all, teachers didn't lose their jobs and redundancy was not their particular lot, or was it?

Deighton was a splendid 'inner-city' establishment but with a fearsome reputation, and many cultures, but to my mind an oasis in the midst of much deprivation and disadvantage. I had had the good fortune to listen to its acting Head, Trevor Coldman, expouse its virtues whilst on a multicultural course in Leeds. Little did I know that some six months later I would successfully capture its Headship.

My interview for the position at Deighton consisted of a day in the centre itself followed the next day by a further interview with the Chair of Governors and senior officers at a Teachers' Centre just out of Huddersfield Town Centre.

Two nerve jangling days but a Chair of Governors who was also a formidable Councillor of real working class stock seemed very much on my side. I think I was his sort of man. Many years later he came to see me at Park Lane to find the truth behind some scandal involving one of my non-teaching staff, scandal of a very serious nature which, if it hadn't been dealt with internally might have led to prosecution or worse.

"Let it go John", I counselled, "Let it go".

Reluctantly, because he was a terrier, he accepted that what was done was done and no good would have come from raking over coals which had gone cold more than a decade previously. I always admired him for that because he was a powerful formidable man – now sadly deceased.

I had only one previous unsuccessful Headship interview before the Deighton one – similar school, similar situation, but it was not to be a controversial return to my home town.

There were not a lot of things to immediately sort out as I inherited a quite dedicated staff used to the diversification of a multicultural ethos (60% Afro-Caribbean, 20% Asian). Surprisingly however they were battling, as a staff, to publicly proclaim their multicultural policy and beliefs. Paradoxically they were actually doing it in their daily teaching and their care of pupils, but for some reason were unable to get this down in writing and prepare a public statement which political correctness was demanding.

Having already formulated a Cockburn multicultural policy (later to be plagiarised as a Leeds CC policy) I waded straight in.

"Please get it together over the next two weeks I urged or my policy will go in."

It worked a treat, and although quite a bit did come from me, it was equally important to recognise that a lot also came from this working party too.

Uniform was another issue here – the dress was a fiasco. Despite warnings I encouraged form tutors – fiercely proud here of their role – to tape discussions about my proposals for dress. I was given the recordings of the uniform debate and the responses of the children and what they had to say was mind boggling.

"Great, we'll all look like we belong somewhere now!"

"If that twat thinks he's getting me into a jumper, shirt and tie he's even more stupid than I think he is."

"We'll look great - just like them Fartown kids." (Fartown was a more respected rival school).

"I'm not dressing up for anybody, let's see him try and make me!"

and so on, and so on….

Well Sir did make 'em. Backed by the staff, the governors and parents on the day of reckoning just twenty four turned up almost in fancy dress!

"Cheerio folks," I said. "Let me know which other school you prefer or better still, see you in appropriate dress."

Next day there were twelve recalcitrants not wearing ties, and by the end of the week, we'd cracked it.

A small but interesting point was made when the girls' representative asked me why they couldn't wear ties! Like the boys!

Terrific – at a stroke the whole school population wore ties.

The first two years were taken up with routine 'new broom' measures but a lot of what the school was about and stood for and what it accomplished as a matter of routine, was good and innovative. It was incredibly strong in sport for a small school, but in the arts, I felt it was depressingly disappointing. Again, any institution is only as good as those teaching individuals in it, and the arts sadly lacked both passion and real commitment.

It was also obvious that the management was male dominated and the appointment – eventually – of a female Deputy Headteacher was a blessing although having given birth to two children in a very short period of time meant two huge time gaps. From the perspective of a fuller development the roll numbers at Deighton had dropped from well in excess of 1000 pupils to about 600 and it took around three years to stop the drain and begin to build up numbers again. Alas, the political climate was against us. As a small school we were easy meat in terms of parent ability to organise and fight the proposed closure. Despite a number upturn, the writing was on the wall.

There were characters at Deighton from top to bottom of the staff strata. I began to develop my bowling skills in a local team where Deighton cleaners, dinner ladies, staff and parents were major elements of the team. This gave me some wonderful after school social nights.

My caretaker was an alcoholic, and he was eventually found dead, wedged behind his front door, after another enormous binge. I recall that when the car-park was newly tarmaced he insisted on putting 'Head' on my space in large white letters. It took a very short time for some wag to prefix it with 'Dick'. Derek was mortified. He always showed me total respect and always referred to me as 'Sir'. However, like so many others, he loved the place and genuinely suffered when it had to go.

Eventually, news came of the possible closure of the school. This time, there was to be no demolition and no destruction. There was to be a development of the school's community and training centre dimension, which was beginning to be developed very successfully alongside the provision of 11 – 16 mandatory education.

I always believed that if the community saw what was happening and were an integral part of this, then the school numbers would improve. This happened of course but too late for the early 1990s era of many school closures.

I should mention we did have a fire in 1989 when the music suite and main hall were gutted.

On New Year's Day night one of my deputies Jim rang to say

'Do you want the good news or the bad news governor?'

Pause.

'The good news please, Jim'.

'There's no need for you to come over but we've had a fire – there's nothing you can do tonight. Happy New Year!'

Can I recommend that all schools have at least one good fire every ten years or so. The new equipment and refurbishment provided had long been overdue and would not have been granted through the normal channels. Seriously, it was demoralising though, particularly for teachers who lost so much personal stuff, not just years of successful lesson preparation but the memorabilia associated with successful teaching. Quite a few came to see me demolished and heartbroken and needing to be very carefully nurtured back to teaching health.

Another interesting story, which did my cause no good at all, was the dumping of some kittens by two members of staff – again during the Christmas holidays. This was an incident which did the school no favours either. One member had taken in, out of pity, an abandoned cat found in a field, but when this gave birth to a litter of kittens, and the latter were old enough, she put the job lot back into the original field accompanied by a friend. Their action was spotted, the car number taken, and the RSPCA duly prosecuted. By the way, I found out this year that the animal authorities do this all the time in India – ie return to place where found once they have been 'doctored'.

The first I knew was when the Deputy C.EO rang me with the news. Local radio made it the second item to the Reagan/Gorbechov meeting in Malta; and the Huddersfield Examiner's headlines claimed 'Deighton teachers dump kittens'. Not 'teachers dump kittens, or Kirklees teachers dump kittens, but Deighton's teachers!

I chastised the Examiner's editor for this, and he saw my point. However, through the years this paper actually did us very proud with positive publicity often to the chagrin of fellow heads. On the matter of the kittens, the two people concerned and my then chair of Governors met at his home to discuss the implications, the possible consequences and the necessary action to be taken. It was after 2.00am in the morning when I left to drive home to Leeds.

After many meetings, protestations, sorting out of retirements, redeployment and general unsettlement the axe finally fell. There was a brief flirtation with grant-maintained status, but as I'd already lost my best staff, I knew that the school was no longer staffed with the sort of people required to kick-start it very quickly. The proportion of 'tired and settled older end' were too many – the dynamos had been transferred to other bikes.

Towards the end my Deputy came in, sat down and said.

"Well we've settled everyone's future Governor, but yours?"

He often used this term most affectionately and I knew that he was a bit bothered by my predicament. However I had another year to consider my future and that seemed like long enough.

Jim got up, reached the office door, turned and said,

"But then Gov. you're a real survivor. I'm not really worried about you, things seem to happen for you."

How prophetic were his words when one year later I obtained work which saw me as happy and fulfilled educationally as I'd ever been, and which was to see me to retirement and beyond.

I spent 1992-1993 doing a masters degree specifically analysing the closure of the school. I pulled no punches, politically it was received with very mixed feelings but it's worth reading and quite another story. Kirklees kindly paid for my course, and I owe them a lot for it certainly helped me overcome the trauma and acted as a catharsis.

The Chairman of Governors and his wife remain very firm and good friends and we frequently meet up – another excellent legacy. In the 1991/92 sports season, the last as a full school, the school netball and rugby teams swept the honours' board beating all the bigger schools along the way. I had looked at us becoming a school of sporting excellence without any success. Ten years later schools of excellence seemed ten a penny, but ten years too late for us!

Another proposal from myself and the Governing Body was the 'through school' ie siting nursery age through to sixteen year olds in the vast half-empty Deighton Secondary building. The Junior School was ailing, the ancient Infant School was falling about the ears of the children, and some imaginative planning and determined organisation by the Education Authority was all it needed. 'Impossible' for the Kirklees administration, 'Roy is clutching at straws' was the enlightened view of the Chief

Education Officer at that time – soon to become another Authority casualty.

So the dream seemed to be ending for me personally. One year of awful in- between meaningless work to retirement. Battles with the greedy, unfeeling and uncaring management of the nearby Secondary School dominated in cavalier fashion.

What sweet music some two years later when a Senior Education Officer – who must remain nameless – said to me –

"Roy, I'll never admit saying this, but we closed the wrong school."

I remember many incidents. Trying to interview a parent who insisted he record our meeting with a huge ghetto blaster. He was given short thrift. Later I overheard him giving my Head of Year some hassle and trying to defend a very naughty young man. Unable to resist I had to step in – something I rarely did.

"Actually can I be blunt Mr Cunningham, Andrew is a total pain in the ass."

Our only problem really was his Dad. Given the chance we could have sorted him out. We were never given that chance and in due course he was excluded. We developed one Home Economics area, not used because of low numbers, into a nursery. The teacher who had worked there from the outset for some forty years or so refused to budge while all around her was demolished, rebuilt and refurbished – she was very akin to the Captain refusing to leave a sinking ship. The advent of twenty sometimes-smelly infants and babies finally persuaded her.

Losing two students to leukemia was a tragic and humbling experience, especially when both parents insisted on providing lasting memorial trusts to the school – gifts they really could scarcely afford – but that was the nature of the parents. A warmer hearted, more giving and generous community it would be difficult to find – they were poor but good people. Twice we exchanged with a German school and finding appropriate and willing homes was not difficult – all at their own added expense of course.

Memories and incidents keep on preventing me finishing my tale, another such one was a visit with my Head of Careers – Mick Peace, a dour Yorkshire man – and several school leavers looking for an army career. Our venue was Strensall Barracks in York.

I declined the sergeant's invitation to try the assault course - crawling around perimeters, jumping fences and trying to climb ropes, or slide through tunnels etc., were not activities I was prepared to undertake (Remember my secondary education's P.E. problems?)

However the sergeant looking after my group, and the students, did persuade me to target practice reluctant though I was to handle a rifle and fire bullets. Flat on my tummy, concentrating manfully, I pumped bullets into the horrific face confronting me through the sights, or so I mistakenly thought.

"How have I done?" I proudly asked the Sergeant.

"Not bad Sir", he replied, "Not bad at all, you've certainly shot tons of sand into his face!"

Mortified, we all went to the officer's mess for lunch and I gained another first experience here - that of whizzing a large decanter of port around the huge dining table. You either stopped it and poured one, or you pushed it on – if you were really clever the decanter never paused. It was a bit difficult listening to the speeches as I was more fascinated by the decanter of port.

The memories will stay with me forever. What now, as at the end of the term in 1993, my prospects of meaningful work seemed dim. There was to be a further intervention by someone up there who certainly understood that at 57, I was still wanting. However 1992/93 gave me the opportunity to obtain a cherished M.Ed.- not that it would be currency of any particular value at this time of my life. I didn't quite know what I perceived for the next stage of my career.

Chapter 10

An Indian Summer in Park Lane

My daughter rang me in that Summer of 1993 when, at 57, I found myself redundant, yet without a mortgage – a lovely feeling – but whoever visualised redundant teachers in the 1970s? Miners yes, steel workers yes, but teachers!

"Dad there's a twelve hour a week job advertised at Park Lane College, tailor made for you in the Drama Department – go for it."

I applied, reinvented my curricular vitae and received some days later a telephone call from the Head of Department.

"Hello, is that the same Roy Norcliffe who was my Chief Moderator in Drama in the early 1980s? This is Vivienne here... remember, I was once part of your team?"

"Yes", I replied cautiously.

"We'd like you to attend for interview but because I know you, I won't be present. Good luck anyway."

On the due date I attended for interview with four other hopefuls all much younger than me - idealistic people not afraid to voice both opinion and experiences. Experiences!! I kept my mouth shut and later that evening received a call saying I had the job. Fantastic. No pressures, do as I was told, didn't need think too deeply, and no management decisions. Well it was nearly all of that. Within days the beautiful female director asked me if I would manage the GCSE programme in Drama.

"It's not usual to ask a part-timer but you are a bit different," she said.

Pauline was often apologising for my lowly status and comparatively low pay but to me it really didn't matter. I was happy at work again. Involved, active and committed, the years flew by.

For the next academic year the College wished to appoint a lecturer for two and a half days a week, but I never considered applying, believing it to be the province of the more modern up to date Drama teachers who were certain to apply.

However again the phone rang and Pauline Waterhouse, the Arts and Sciences Director came straight to the point asking why I had not applied?

"Age, a bit behind the modern Drama teaching techniques and technology," I countered.

"But rich in so many other educational areas – please apply."

Words which again had a momentous knock-on effect, because I did apply, and I was successful. Thus my self-worth and esteem-shaken quite badly by the 1992/93 fracas – were fully restored. So Pauline became yet another human being providentially sent my way by 'someone up there'. She was to have a profound effect on my next seven working years before the age of 65, when I would hopefully retire.

I was to discover that the next seven years or so were to become the most exciting and fulfilling of my chequered and unusual career. In point of fact when I retired from the College, I had spent more time in the place than I'd spent in any post since leaving school.

I continued to lead the GCSE Drama programme, realising that I hadn't lost my touch with some outstanding results. I don't want to appear immodest but the fact that I could still achieve success – often with very limited but worthy young people – was gratifying and truly rewarding.

I taught on BTEC programmes, First Diploma courses and developed strong community links with agencies such as senior citizens homes, hospitals, schools and on a regular basis produced historical pieces of theatre in the Leeds museums and Armley Mills, the Armouries and the Thackery Hospital Museum respectively. Indeed to this day we have continued the link with the Armley Mills and each Christmas perform in this beautiful and atmospheric old building to the general public and to visiting school parties.

Some of the work was sobering, and once performing to very young children in a cancer ward, the general commotion in a far corner of the ward was a result of the death of a young patient. My students working in a very tight space, surrounded by eager young faces and a truly receptive audience were so focused that they were unaware at the time of the tragedy. The gravity came home to them when grieving parents were being comforted in the room where they had changed and left their clothes. After eventually retrieving these it was a sombre group of young people who returned to college still in costume and mostly in tears.

It was a painful life lesson and I was always full of admiration for my students whenever after that we tackled other hospital wards where their work gave such undisguised pleasure to the children.

Only two years or so ago I was reminded of my time in the self-same ward when one of my own Granddaughters was diagnosed with a brain tumour, aged 13, she was visited this time by professional entertainers. It lifted all the children's' spirits and also the spirits of we parents and Grandparents. Ainsley Harriott was particularly incredible in the way he approached these young people. His charisma, energy and sheer presence was inspirational. Whilst I'm not pretending our children's' shows in any way matched this, it was good to know that through Drama and improvisation, we made some worthwhile impressions.

After two years of delivering these routine programmes I was unexpectedly called upon to work on a brand new course in Tourism and Travel. This was to develop students in the world of holidays, entertainment representatives etc. and was entitled Travel and Tourism (animateur option). I understand that when my name was put forward as the Performance Arts lecturer – there were doubts expressed in high places. Doubts, simply because I refused to work on Mondays! (my wife June also had free Mondays it gave us long weekends, another excellent late career bonus).

However my line manager in Performing Arts suggested I was approached and the brand new course with an enthusiastic, if temporarily uncertain, team in terms of course content, tackled the work with real gusto. Those of my readers who have planned and plotted new courses probably had someone or something they could refer to – not us. However, we did work alongside similarly like-minded institutions as Consortia centres in Ireland, Dundee,

Belgium, France and Majorca in particular, but one by one they withdrew as the September of 1996 deadline drew nigh. We had no need to worry, and with other institutions hanging on our coat-tail, we delivered a tremendously exciting course at advanced level. In recent years, this has been delivered as Advanced Diploma Units. Excellent stepping stones for a career in entertainment, travel or indeed University.

At the same time – almost by chance – my European responsibilities naturally evolved within the Performing Arts Department. Whilst working for both departments I was privileged to visit Finland (twice), Ireland (twice), Rhodes, Crete, Greece (twice), Spain (twice), Dundee, Brussels, Ibiza, and Budapest. Additionally, the college linked with Thompson's holiday company and I was given a terrific insight into their recruitment policies, their auditioning and initial training techniques – matters which were tremendously exciting to feed back to our Leeds students. The year after I officially 'retired', I began an association in Malta where we had a holiday home, an association which, sadly, only lasted two years. As I write, the European link-up in the Performing Arts Department is nil, excuses being that since Roy left, no-one has the time. I refer to my theme 'there's nowt like wanting'.

My book 'There and Back Again' refers to educational experiences in Malta but two long term visits to Ireland and Finland, where we toured some children's theatre, will live in my memory for ever. Again the trials and tribulations encountered in Ireland have been documented in 'There and Back Again' where it was the sheer inhospitability of our hosts which perversely made the jaunt worthwhile, and the way in which the students coped with adversity and illness to provide ultimately stunning theatre. Finland was a different ball game. Fifteen students and our staff (in alternate twos) spent three weeks coping with temperatures in the region of -20°C in the February of 1998. Again, Children's' Theatre was presented to schools and colleges and even to nurseries. By Children's' Theatre we mean entertaining plays, but plays conveying an educational or perhaps serious environmental issue.

My co-staff member was Glynis, a compassionate caring colleague who suited the demands made by a group of young people often from disadvantaged and deprived backgrounds, all endeavouring to catch up on years of educational struggle and late educational development. Memories abound such as the staff change over night when we embarked on a Kotka pub-crawl, encountering a look-alike, sound-alike, of Les Dawson; Glynis leaving the swimming pool with wet hair and it transforming into a head of icicles before she reached our car.

The students usually made it to the various venues by public transport, i.e. the local bus and it was great to see them persuading the driver to take our backcloth and either lay it in the bus or to store it in the luggage compartment. They always negotiated successfully this bit under their own steam – another learning process.

We were given the opportunity to wind-sail on the frozen lakes and sea, to ski and to ice-skate – experiences mainly unlikely back in Yorkshire. Perhaps the funniest occasion was one Saturday night when the students asked if they could go into town to celebrate a 17th birthday party. Kotka was in North East Finland only a comparatively short distance from the Russian border and it was, as I've said, bitterly cold – and still only February.

We were based in a beautiful period Youth Hostel by the lakeside and on this particular night many of the students tarted themselves up in flimsy summer gear with high heels for the girls and open neck shirts for the boys. Glynis and I gazed in disbelief as they all filed passed and disappeared to tackle the hundred-yard snow covered walk to the bus stop.

"How long?" asked Glynis.

"Five minutes," I hazarded a guess.

Sure enough after maybe six minutes all returned either having fallen, been frost-bitten or worse.

"Why not keep all your lovely clothes on, put your shoes into plastic bags, cover up with coats, scarves, hats and gloves and take 'em all off when you get there?" we suggested. Needless to say, they complied – another learning curve.

So life at Park Lane suddenly turned into perhaps the happiest and meaningful period of my career, European work, routine work, academic success. The heartaches of my school closure had become a distant memory.

I was also offered some work with disillusioned and disaffected Year 11 pupils, excluded from their respective schools, but offered an educational lifeline by the college. Hand on heart, this wasn't too successful mainly because of absences. Paradoxically however, some Drama work with young people with profound learning difficulties was hugely successful. I recruited an actress friend, formally a student of mine, and Claire proved a beautiful and gifted support teacher.

Thus 65 approached, and my last key role for Park Lane was the development of a HND Theatre and Drama course to begin September 2001. I enjoyed this academic challenge particularly when my Friday afternoon classes were farmed out and for the first time in years I could go home early.

The teacher taking these GCSE classes was also a theatrical agent who persuaded me to consider doing TV 'extra' work for his agency – something I still do – although only occasionally as I'm busy and thus unavailable.

I referred earlier to Pauline Waterhouse, the Director at that time of Arts and Sciences. Not only was Pauline very beautiful but she was also extremely able and a tremendous manager. She frequently motivated, was thorough in understanding people, their strengths and weaknesses, and not afraid to tap into my own considerable management expertise when she felt it worthwhile to do so.

One year a show at Kirkstall Abbey, 'Jesus Christ Superstar', resulted in the young man playing Judas suffering an injury during the 'hanging scene' which might have been fatal had the rope not been a ring but a noose. It was actually support harness failure, but the press got hold of the story and my job was to field the National press. Our own Health and Safety Officials were obviously in their element. Thus Health and Safety henceforth became a key issue in all our productions, visits at home and abroad, and in the classroom. The memos and directions flew everywhere and one day Pauline decided to give us all a pep talk and minor rollicking.

She was wearing a light blue two-piece on the day in question and I couldn't help but notice and admire not only her delivery, but her beauty. She finished her tirade, there was a silence and then she asked the team if there were any questions.

I said, "Pauline, may I say something please?."

"Yes, what is it,?" she snapped.

"Can I just say that you look absolutely stunning in that blue outfit!"

I just couldn't resist it and realised then the value of age and security.

On another occasion in the office she shared with the assistant Director she was giving me hard time about someone else's shortcomings. After a while seeing my face and after hearing me say several times, "Pauline I'll sort it", she came round to the front of her desk and threw her arms around me.

"Why, oh why, am I giving you of all people a hard time, you've been a manager, you know the difficulties" etc. etc…

I picked her up; she was very tiny (obviously) and spun her around two or three times to the stunned amazement of the Assistant Director seated at his desk. Murmuring suitable platitudes, I left the office! I couldn't have been more delighted and proud that this woman spoke so highly of me at my presentation do, because I should have also mentioned that she monitored one of our visits to Southern Greece and was a delightful and supportive colleague respected and admired by the staff and the students she accompanied.

Thus in July 2001 my official 'working' life had come to an end but there was still sufficient petrol in the tank to see out a few other interesting plans.

CHAPTER 11

'Bits and Bobs'

From 2001 to the present time I engaged myself in occasional work at Park Lane via an agency and in particular saw through the first three years of the new HND course. Sadly this wasn't to prove successful and was modified in 2004.

I also became a Drama examiner for several units at 'A' Level and now lead a team of five examiners, I continued GCSE moderation until 2004 for the Oxford and Cambridge Examination Board and continued my Thursday morning Animateur work, until 2005. The end of year celebratory cabaret moved from College presentation onto a local working-men's club, and is now annually installed at the famous Leeds City Varieties. This is a fitting and stunning showcase for the students' final work.

Thus my 'work' is confined to examination times only, February to June, although I term it 'retirement interests' for whom someone wishes to pay me! There is a difference; there again, my time in education since 1971 has never seemed like 'work'. Lucky me.

Throughout my life, when I have wanted something, I've 'gone for it' and usually got it. Things were to change however, when in October 2004, my father died at the age of ninety-five. His retirement lasted thirty years and apart from the last few months of his long life he was extremely fit, and very alert.

A couple of days or so before he died he called myself and my sister to his bedside to tell us we 'were hopeless!" Whether he meant it in terms of our lives or because we couldn't hasten his end, we weren't quite sure – we trusted it was the latter as he'd become very frustrated at his incapacities. When he was first admitted to the Macmillan Unit in Sheffield's Northern General Hospital Palliative care ward, he was questioned about his life, and despite it being an effort, we recorded the following facts. All of this was written up with a community welfare worker, anxious that some of his past not be lost forever, and to give him some mental stimulation too. The following is what she was told by Dad.

JAMES ARTHUR NORCLIFFE, BORN 21ST DECEMBER 1908 – DIED OCTOBER 3RD 2004

"WORKING AND HAVING A FAMILY MADE LIFE WORTH LIVING."

"JIM'S DAUGHTER WILL BE COMING BACK FROM HOLIDAY ON SUNDAY."

"JIM'S DAUGHTER RECOVERING FROM A BREAST OPERATION – HIS SON IS GOING ON HOLIDAY TO FRANCE TOMORROW."

"JIM HAS HAD A CARD OR TELEPHONE CALL EVERY DAY FROM HIS DAUGHTER."

JIM WORKED IN THE PIT FOR FIFTY YEARS, THIRTY-EIGHT AS AN UNDERGROUND COLLIERY OVERMAN OFFICIAL. HE SUPERVISED PEOPLE MINING AT SMITHY WOOD COLLIERY. THIS WAS AT THORPE

HESLEY IN 1947. EVERY COLLIERY LOST ITS NAME AND BECAME NCB COLLIERIES."

"JIM WAS 15 WHEN HE WENT DOWN THE PIT."

"HE HAD BEEN TO SCHOOL AT THORPE HESLEY JUNIOR SCHOOL."

"JIM'S FATHER WANTED HIM TO GO ON THE FARM – HIS FATHER WORKED IN THE MINE – BUT DIDN'T WANT JIM TO FOLLOW HIM AND HIS BROTHERS. (HE RECEIVED PUNISHMENT WHEN HIS FATHER FOUND OUT)"

"JIM HAD THREE BROTHERS AND FIVE SISTERS – JOHN, SAMUEL, GEORGE, FLORENCE, FRANCES, JIM, SALLY, ELIZABETH, (BESSIE), AND MADGE, AND OUTLIVED THEM ALL . HE ALSO OUTLIVED ALL OF HIS BROTHERS AND SISTERS IN LAW."

"ELDEST SISTERS FLORENCE & FRANCES WORKED AT JOHN WALSH'S BEFORE THE WAR. IT WAS A LARGE SHOP IN SHEFFIELD LIKE ATKINSONS. IT WAS DAMAGED. THEY HAD TO MOVE IN THE BLITZ. THEY MOVED FROM HIGH ST. TO ELSEWHERE IN SHEFFIELD. JIM WORKED ON A FARM FOR TWO YEARS. IT WAS A FAMILY FARM NEXT DOOR TO WHERE HE LIVED. HE DID EVERYTHING THERE - PLOUGHING, MOWING, REAPING, SOWING, AND MILKING. HE ENJOYED IT BUT THOUGHT THE MINE WOULD BE A LITTLE BIT MORE REMUNERATIVE. THERE WAS MORE OPPORTUNITY IN THE MINE, THUS HE WENT DOWN THE PIT FOR FINANCIAL REASONS."

"HE HAD QUITE A LOT OF GOOD FRIENDS THERE. ODD ONES KEPT IN TOUCH. MR ARTHUR AUSTIN,

WHO LIVED IN THORPE HESLEY, STAYED CLOSE FRIENDS WITH JIM FOR SEVENTY YEARS OR MORE. THEY WERE FOOTBALL FRIENDS. HE AND HIS SON USED TO CALL FOR JIM AND TAKE HIM TO FOOTBALL AND BRING HIM HOME SAFELY."

"HE SUPPORTED SHEFFIELD WEDNESDAY – WENT TO HILLSBOROUGH. ARTHUR DIED IN 1993. HIS SON DECIDED HE WAS PACKING UP (HE USED TO TRANSPORT THEM) – JIM SAID 'IF YOU ARE PACKING UP JOHN, SO WILL I" - HE NEVER WENT AGAIN. NOW HIS SON ROY KEEPS HIM INFORMED. HE LISTENS TO RADIO, WATCHES MATCHES ON T.V. AND FOLLOWS THE TEAM IN THE "STAR."

JIM GOT MARRIED 1934 APRIL 5TH. FULWOOD PARISH CHURCH. ELSIE LIVED AT FULWOOD. THEY MET AT A WHIST DRIVE AT FULWOOD. A FRIEND TOOK HIM THERE. JIM WAS 25 AND ELSIE WAS 29. COURTING FOR FOUR YEARS."

"THEY SET UP HOUSE IN ECCLESFIELD. ELSIE WORKED AT NORTH EAST MIDLAND PRESCRIPTION BUREAU ON GLOSSOP ROAD. SHE STOPPED WORK WHEN THEY GOT MARRIED. THEY LIVED TOGETHER IN THE SAME HOUSE FOR FORTY-THREE YEARS. THEY HAD A FAMILY – SON ROY IN 1936, DAUGHTER JILLIAN IN 1938,"

JIM HAS FOUR GRANDCHILDREN. MARK, BEVERLY, ANDREW, AND DAVID. MARK IS MARRIED TO ZITA AND HIS FIRST GREAT-GRANDCHILD IS FAYE. BEVERLEY IS MARRIED TO GARY AND THEY HAVE THREE CHILDREN, NATALIE, CHARLOTTE

AND BRADLEY. ANDREW IS MARRIED TO IMOGEN AND THEY HAVE THREE CHILDREN, REUBEN, AYSHA, AND MATHEW. MATHEW IS THE YOUNGEST GREAT GRANDCHILD, JIM'S OLDEST GRAND-DAUGHTER, FAYE, WILL BE TWENTY-ONE IN SEPTEMBER. ROY IS MARRIED TO JUNE, AND JILLIAN IS MARRIED TO GEOFF.

(back to his teenage working years now)

"DID YOU WORK WITH A HORSE?"

"COULDN'T DO IT WITHOUT, LOVE."

HAD FOUR HORSES, BUT JIM USED THREE (THE FARMER USED THE FOURTH.) THEIR NAMES WERE BLOSSOM, BULLER AND KICKER – BECAUSE IT KICKED A LOT. CHOSE BULLER FOR PLOUGHING. HAD TWO HORSES TOGETHER FOR PLOUGHING.

JIM LOOKED AFTER THE HORSES.

ELSIE'S PARENTS WON A CARVING SET IN A PLOUGHING MATCH IN FULWOOD. THEY ARE STILL IN USE EVERY SUNDAY AT JILLIAN'S HOUSE.

JIM GOT FINED FOR SPEEDING ON HIS MOTORCYCLE IN 1929 AT LAUGHTON COMMON CROSSROADS – NEAR SWALLOWNEST. HE WAS FINED TEN SHILLINGS, (OR FIFTY P), FOR SPEEDING. JIM WAS 21 YEARS OLD.

IN 1950 COMING BACK FROM WATCHING BURNLEY PLAYING SHEFFIELD WEDNESDAY IN THE SNOW, THEY GOT DIVERTED OVER WOODHEAD PASS. THEY HAD TO GET OUT OF THE COACH AND PUSH IT ROUND A DOUBLE 'S' BEND ON THE WAY DOWN – POLICE REFUSED TO LET JIM AND A FRIEND GET OUT AND SCATTER ASHES. THEY SAID "DON'T WORRY, WE'RE

IN GOOD HANDS – WE ARE ALL FIRST AIDERS." FROM AN AFTERNOON MATCH AT BLACKBURN , IT TOOK US ABOUT TWELVE HOURS TO GET HOME (dad kept saying Blackburn but it was in fact Burnley – I was with him!)

"1935 WEDNESDAY WON F.A. CUP, 1991 RUMBELOW'S CUP (1966 AND 1993 THEY WERE IN THE FINAL). 1993 IN TWO FINALS. THE 1935 TEAM WAS BROWN, WALKER, BLENKINSOP, SHARP, MILLERSHIP, BURROUGHS, HOOPER, SURTEES, PALETHORPE, STARLING, RIMMER. GOALS SCORED BY MARK HOOPER – 2 –, AND ELLIS RIMMER – 2 AGAINST WEST BROMWICH ALBION. PLAYED AT WEMBLEY". JIM COULD NOT GET A TICKET. HE WENT IN 66' – THEY PLAYED EVERTON, AND IN 1991 WHEN THEY BEAT MANCHESTER UNITED.

(Recorded August 29th and September 9th 2004)

How we all 'wanted' to help dad at the end of his long life, but how powerless we were. We wanted him to live but couldn't extend his life. Sometimes, in spite of however much we want something, we cannot get it. I trust that you, my reader, will be discerning enough to accept that there are a range of differences on the ' wanting' scale.

A number of 'ifs' thread through this story! What 'if' in1971, the evening school Head in Sheffield hadn't taken the time and trouble to guide me into the teaching profession? What 'if' I hadn't been approached by The Deputy Head at Garforth in 1974? What 'if' my daughter hadn't seen the advertisement in the local paper which drew me to Park Lane College; and the Director there, who rang me advising me to apply for the Performing Arts post when it was up for grabs? Certainly fate played a major part in all of this and provided much to reflect upon in retirement.

Printed in the United Kingdom
by Lightning Source UK Ltd.
114564UKS00001B/184-204